The Development of the Alternative Black Curriculum, 1890–1940

Alana D. Murray

The Development of the Alternative Black Curriculum, 1890–1940

Countering the Master Narrative

palgrave
macmillan

Alana D. Murray
Montgomery County Public Schools
Rockville, MD, USA

ISBN 978-3-030-08249-9   ISBN 978-3-319-91418-3 (eBook)
https://doi.org/10.1007/978-3-319-91418-3

© The Editor(s) (if applicable) and The Author(s) 2018
Softcover re-print of the Hardcover 1st edition 2018
This work is subject to copyright. All rights are solely and exclusively licensed by the Publisher, whether the whole or part of the material is concerned, specifically the rights of translation, reprinting, reuse of illustrations, recitation, broadcasting, reproduction on microfilms or in any other physical way, and transmission or information storage and retrieval, electronic adaptation, computer software, or by similar or dissimilar methodology now known or hereafter developed.
The use of general descriptive names, registered names, trademarks, service marks, etc. in this publication does not imply, even in the absence of a specific statement, that such names are exempt from the relevant protective laws and regulations and therefore free for general use.
The publisher, the authors, and the editors are safe to assume that the advice and information in this book are believed to be true and accurate at the date of publication. Neither the publisher nor the authors or the editors give a warranty, express or implied, with respect to the material contained herein or for any errors or omissions that may have been made. The publisher remains neutral with regard to jurisdictional claims in published maps and institutional affiliations.

Cover image © John Frost Newspapers / Alamy Stock Photo
Cover design by Fatima Jamadar

Printed on acid-free paper

This Palgrave Macmillan imprint is published by the registered company Springer International Publishing AG part of Springer Nature.
The registered company address is: Gewerbestrasse 11, 6330 Cham, Switzerland

*This book is dedicated to Rosa Walker Murray, Margery Prout, and Edna Louise Rice.
My grandmothers exemplified education for liberation and raised a community built on love.*

A TIMELINE OF THE DEVELOPMENT OF THE ALTERNATIVE BLACK CURRICULUM IN SOCIAL STUDIES, 1890–1940

1892	*A Voice from the South* is written by Anna Julia Cooper
1894	*The Work of the Afro-American Women* is written by Gertrude E.H. Bustill
1904	Mary McLeod Bethune founded the Daytona Educational and Industrial Training Institute for Negro Girls
1909	Nannie H. Burroughs founded the National Training School for Women and Girls
1911	*The Star of Ethiopia* is written by W.E.B. Du Bois
1912	*A Narrative of the Negro* is written by Leila Amos Pendleton
1915	Carter G. Woodson established the Association for the Study of Negro Life and History
1916	*The Journal of Negro History* is established by Carter G. Woodson
1917	*Douglass Pageant: A Pageant in Honor of His Centenary* is written and produced by Alice Dunbar Nelson
1919	*Missing Pages in American History: Revealing the Services of Negroes in the Early Wars of the United States of America* is written by Laura Eliza Wilkes
	A Short History of the American Negro is published by Benjamin Griffith Brawley
1920–1921	*The Brownies' Book* is published; Jessie Redmond Fauset and W.E.B. Du Bois are co-editors
1921	*When Truth Gets a Hearing* (pageant) is written by Nannie H. Burroughs
	Unsung Heroes is published by Elizabeth Ross Haynes
1922	*The Negro in Our History* is written by Carter G. Woodson
	Two Races (pageant) is written by Inez Burke
	The International Council of the Women of the Darker Races (ICWDR) is formed by Margaret Murray Washington
1923	The Daytona and Industrial Institute school becomes Bethune-Cookman College

1924	Mary McLeod Bethune becomes the President of the National Association of Negro Women (NACW)
	Out of the Dark (pageant) is written by Dorothy C. Guinn
1926	Negro History Week established by Carter G. Woodson
1929	*When Truth Gets a Hearing* is performed at the Association for Negro Life and History
1929	*Graven Images* (pageant) is written and produced by May Miller
1930	*Plays and Pageants from the Life of the Negro* is published by Carter G. Woodson
	The Light of the Women (pageant) is written and by Frances Gunner
1932	*Historical Pageant-Play Based on the Life of Phyllis [sic] Wheatley* is written by Mary Church Terrell
	George Washington and Black Folk: A Pageant for the Bicentennial, 1732–1932 is written by W.E.B. Du Bois
1933	*The Mis-Education of the Negro* is published by Carter G. Woodson
1935	*Forward* (play) is written and produced by Washington DC school teacher, Louise Lovett
	Black Reconstruction in America: An Essay Toward a History of the Part Which Black Folk Played in the Attempt to Reconstruct Democracy in America, 1860–1880 is written by W.E.B. Du Bois
1936	Mary McLeod Bethune becomes president of ASNLH
1937	*The Negro History Bulletin* is established
	A Guide to the Study of the Negro in American History is written by Merl R. Eppse
1938	*Jungle Lore* is written by Louise Lovett
	The Negro, Too, in American History is written by Merl R. Eppse
1939	*An Elementary History of America, Including the Contributions of the Negro Race* is written with A.P. Foster
1940	*From Servitude to Service, Contributions from the Negro Peoples in American History: A Pageant* is written by Anna Julia Cooper
1942	Madeline Morgan Stratton creates a comprehensive black history curriculum in Chicago Public Schools. (Supplementary Units for a Course in Social Studies)
	Mary Church Terrell writes "Pageant-Play Depicting Heroism of Colored Soldiers in Revolutionary War" (n.d.)

Acknowledgments

This book represents the final step of my journey that began during my doctoral studies at the University of Maryland. I began this work under the thoughtful guidance of my advisor, Dr. Victoria-María MacDonald. Dr. MacDonald taught me how to be an education historian and for that I am forever in her debt.

After completing my doctoral journey, I was without an intellectual community. I am particularly grateful for my colleagues Dr. Christine Woyshner and Dr. LaGarrett King. Their thoughtful and insightful comments helped shaped the direction of this particular manuscript. I am also thankful for the friendship of my co-founder in the Equity and Excellence certificate program, Dr. Heather Yuhaniak. Our commitment to creating a program for teachers focused on social justice has truly been a highlight of my educational career. In compiling the final manuscript, the keen editorial eye of Sara Shays assisted me in compiling the final manuscript. I continue to be indebted to Deborah Menkart and Dr. Jenice View as they mentored me in my first opportunity serve as co-editor of the book, *Putting the Movement Back into Civil Rights Teaching*.

Currently, I serve as the "Proud Principal" of Shady Grove Middle School. The opportunity to lead a school connects me with the founders of the alternative black curriculum in profound ways. I would like to thank the students, staff, and community for their support of my work.

During the publication of this book, my beloved grandmothers, Rosa Walker Murray and Edna Louise Rice, passed. Both teachers, my grandmothers, taught me the importance of education for liberation. My dear friend, Tennille D. Holland, and my stepsister, Marona Graham Bailey, also died as I compiled this book. I miss them dearly.

My friends have been the touchstone in my life. Kia Davis, Heather Davis, Cescili Hopkins, Charmaine Flanagan, Erika May, Erica Rossi, Sunny Pippens, Nicole Vaughn, Sharon Cohen, Carrie Booth, Abbey Schneider, Donnice Brown, Kimberly Prillman, Shawaan Robinson, Alison Serino, and Freda Lin have been my rocks touchstones. My dog companion Shinnobi Cleopatra Blue has been a quiet and happy life force. My cousins Veronica Hill, Marvin Hill, Morgan Murray, Sean Murray, and Christina Swann Newby have been great friends to me during our childhood. My stepsiblings Kobie Nettles, Malaika Graham Bailey, Robey Graham Bailey, and Rance Graham Bailey shared my intellectual passion for black history. My church family, Madison Avenue Presbyterian Church, prayed for me as I went through this process. The sisterhood and community of Delta Sigma Theta, Inc. has sustained me as I wrote this book.

The Murrays, the Rices, the Franklins, the Baileys, and the Blues are exemplars of how African American families supported their children through slavery, segregation, and contemporary times. My stepchildren, Tashon I. Blue and Tatyana Blue, supported me as I balanced being a principal and a writer. My stepparents, Ronald Bailey and Lucy Franklin, and my brother-in-law, Dutch Igoni, are wonderful friends who supported me wholeheartedly. My parents, Donald G. Murray, Jr. and Saundra Murray Nettles, amaze me. They both have made a deep commitment to sustaining the African American community, while encouraging and nurturing my personal development. I cherish our conversations.

My twin sister Kali N. Murray is my rock. She provided me with crucial editorial feedback as I shaped my final manuscript. She is a brilliant academic scholar and I am indebted to her. I am so blessed to have had her company in every stage of my life. In addition, she is the proud mother of Saunders Gaines Tolly Murray, who is the provider of joy in our family.

My husband, Mr. Khalif Blue, is my constant. I appreciate his love and support in my work as a school leader and writer. I wake up each day with smile because I know that I am truly loved and cared for. Thank you.

Contents

1 Introduction   1

2 Moving Beyond Biography: Critical Race Theory and the Construction of the Alternative Black Curriculum in Social Studies   13

3 Black Curriculum in Social Studies: A Textual Reading of *When Truth Gets a Hearing*   43

4 Resisting the Master Narrative: Building the Alternative Black *Counter-Canon*   61

5 Exploring the Purposes and Foundations of Black Teacher Preparation: 1890–1940   91

6 Dialogical Spaces: Innovative Practices and the Development of the Alternative Black Curriculum in Social Studies, 1890–1940   107

7 Conclusion	127
References	135
Index	141

List of Figures

Fig. 2.1	Fourth Annual Appreciation Day. (Nannie H. Burroughs, Papers of Nannie H. Burroughs, Library of Congress *Appreciation Day Program,* Box 312)	14
Fig. 2.2	Take your professional temperature quiz. (Nannie H. Burroughs, Papers of Nannie H. Burroughs, Library of Congress, *Take Your Professional Temperature*, undated, Box 311)	25
Fig. 2.3	Our music—"We Sing at this School." (Nannie H. Burroughs, Papers of Nannie H. Burroughs, Library of Congress, *Our Music,* undated, Box 312)	28
Fig. 2.4	How we have been helped by Negro history. (Nannie H. Burroughs, Papers of Nannie H. Burroughs, Library of Congress, Box 312)	30
Fig. 2.5	Ancient history. (Nannie H. Burroughs, Papers of Nannie H. Burroughs, Library of Congress, *History Tests,* 1920–1921, Box 311)	33
Fig. 2.6	US history exams. (Nannie H. Burroughs, Papers of Nannie H. Burroughs, Library of Congress, *History Tests,* 1920–1921, Box 311)	34
Fig. 2.7	English, history, geography, and arithmetic classes. (Burroughs, Nannie H. Papers of Nannie H. Burroughs, Library of Congress, *History Tests,* 1920–1921, Box 311)	35
Fig. 2.8	Double V. (Nannie H. Burroughs, Papers of Nannie H. Burroughs, Library of Congress, *The Negro Project by Miss Gloria Dunlap,* Box 166)	37

Fig. 2.9   Breaking down racial prejudice (The Negro Project).
             (Nannie H. Burroughs, Papers of Nannie H. Burroughs,
             Library of Congress, *Breaking down Racial Prejudice*, Box 166)   38
Fig. 2.10   The past and present history of Germany. (Nannie
             H. Burroughs, Papers of Nannie H. Burroughs, Library of
             Congress, *The Past and Present History of Germany by Miss
             Lorraine Shearron*, Box 166)   39
Fig. 3.1   *When Truth Gets a Hearing* (addition). (Nannie
             H. Burroughs, Papers of Nannie H. Burroughs, Library of
             Congress, *The Past and Present History of Germany by Miss
             Lorraine Shearron*, Box 166)   45

CHAPTER 1

Introduction

In 1912, a textbook for black children, entitled *A Narrative of the Negro*, appeared. We do not know much information about its author, Leila Amos Pendleton. What we do know about her comes from her marriage to Robert Pendleton, a publisher, who owned R. L. Publishing Company. We know that Mrs. Pendleton, as she was known, taught briefly in the Washington DC school system and left her career as a teacher to become a writer. Indeed, Mrs. Pendleton's career change would not have been possible without her fortuitous marriage, as she was also afforded the opportunity to publish her work through her husband's publishing company. Mrs. Pendleton had a relative freedom to write that many black women did not have during the early twentieth century. Mrs. Pendleton also wrote *An Alphabet for Negro Children* (1915), *Our New Possession—the Dutch West Indies* (1917), *An Autobiography of Frederick Douglass* (1921), and two short stories published in the National Association for the Advancement of Colored People (NAACP) magazine *The Crisis*. Mrs. Pendleton remains largely unknown to the public and to subsequent scholars because she lived in an insular, protected community of educated black elites centered in Washington, DC. However, outside of that community, Mrs. Pendleton's work impacted the development of a social studies curriculum that shaped the identity of black children in public schools.

Jessie Redmon Fauset is often described as a "literary" midwife in the blossoming of the Harlem Renaissance. And unlike Mrs. Pendleton, we do know a great deal about Jessie Redmon Fauset. She began her teaching career at Douglass High School in Baltimore, MD, and ended it at DeWitt Clinton High School in New York. Deeply enmeshed in the literary scene of New York, she allied herself philosophically with the "New Negro" movement permeating the black community in the 1920s. Jessie Fauset made significant contributions to the literature of the period authoring four books: *There is Confusion* (1932), *Plum Bun* (1929), *The Chinaberry Tree* (1931), and *Comedy: American Style* (1933), as well as serving as the co-editor of *The Brownies' Book*, a children's literary magazine. Her positive review of Mrs. Pendleton's *A Narrative of the Negro* was published in the *The Crisis* and captures what is known about the response to the textbook, "For this book treats not only of the Negro in the United States, but imaginable way by every nation on every continent, the Negro still is."[1]

Both Mrs. Pendleton and Jessie Fauset combined scholarly pursuits with the more mundane work of being a public-school teacher. As we delve deeper into their stories, we find that Leila Amos Pendleton and Jessie Redmon Fauset share many commonalities beyond simply their professional experiences. These women were part of a small cadre of black women educators who sought to reshape how black children understood the history of African Americans in the United States. They tended to the larger needs of institution building that black communities confronted in the period after Reconstruction, both serving as club women. And both women advocated for a rich view of African American history which combatted a one-dimensional and often racist story generated by white historians.

Several elements of these shared commitments, in many respects, have been studied and recorded within the relevant historical literature. For instance, the comprehensive nature of black women's creation of and participation in the women's club movement is well documented.[2] However, there are other elements of these shared commitments that have been less

---

[1] Jessie Fauset, "What to Read," *The Crisis* 4, no. 4 (August 1912): 1–52.

[2] Evelyn Brooks Higginbotham, *Righteous Discontent: The Women's Movement in the Black Baptist Church 1880–1920* (Cambridge: Harvard University Press, 1993). Deborah Gray White, *Too Heavy a Load, Black Women in Defense of Themselves 1894–1994* (New York: W.W. Norton, 1999). Rosalyn Terborg-Penn, *African American Women in the Struggle to Vote, 1850–1920* (Bloomington: Indiana University Press, 1998). Stephanie J. Shaw. "Black Club Women and the Creation of the National Association of Colored Women." *Journal of Women's History* 3, no. 2 (1991): 11–25. https://muse.jhu.edu/ (accessed December 11, 2017).

studied. This book will examine one of the lesser understood elements of the women's shared commitment: how black women educators sought to create a pedagogical counter-narrative to reframe often-racist national and international education curricula to provide a more accurate rendering of US and world history in the United States. This counter-narrative, which I term the *alternative black curriculum*, refers to the ongoing relationship between the theoretical principles that arose out of institutional contexts of the university and national professional associations and the practical context of the everyday classroom. The basic principles of the alternative black curriculum were often first publicly articulated by male scholars but were subsequently supplemented and even furthered by an ongoing dialogue regarding the pedagogical work of African American women school founders, administrators, librarians, and teachers.[3]

The alternative black curriculum comprises both the content and pedagogy these educators used to implement the curriculum and emphasized four key elements. First, the alternative black curriculum stressed that African civilizations contributed to an overall world history. Second, the curriculum stressed the central role enslaved people played in building social, political, and economic institutions in the United States. Third, the writers of the alternative black curriculum encouraged an identity connected to the African diaspora which linked African American's struggle with people of color throughout the world. Fourth, the alternative black curriculum stressed the needed dialogue about race and racism and the importance of white allies.[4]

My analysis of the alternative black curriculum through the development of educational theory and curriculum during the Progressive Era

---

[3] In each of these texts, authors used terms such as "historical memory" or the "black history narrative" to describe the narrative that I refer to as the alternative black curriculum in social studies. Pero Gaglo Dagbovie, "Making Black History Practical and Popular: Carter G. Woodson, the Proto Black Studies Movement, and the Struggle for Black Liberation," *The Western of Journal of Black Studies* 28 (2004): 372–382. Anthony Brown, "Counter-memory and Race: An Examination of African-American Scholars' Challenges in Early Twentieth Century K-12 Historical Discourse," *The Journal of Negro Education* 79 (Winter 2010): 55–63. Stephen G. Hall, *A Faithful Account of the Race: African American Historical Writing in Nineteenth Century America* (Chapel Hill: University of North Carolina Press, 2009). Jeffrey Aaron Snyder, "Race, Nation and Education: Black History during Jim Crow" (PhD diss., New York University, 2011).

[4] Alana D. Murray, Considerations on the Alternative Black Curriculum in Social Studies: The Book of the Negroes," *The Journal of Social Studies Research* 40, no.1 (January 2016): 1–2.

combines insights from two disciplines, black history and educational history. The absence of black women historians is widely acknowledged with greater attention being focused on the work of Carter G. Woodson and the formation of the Association for the Study of Negro Life and History.[5] In the book *Telling Histories: Black Women Historians in the Ivory Tower*, Deborah Gray White outlines specific ordeals black women confronted in training to become historians and contribute to institutions of higher learning.

The book, *The Development of the Alternative Black Curriculum, 1890–1940: Countering the Master Narrative*, opens several new avenues in its concentration on the alternative black curriculum by employing under-utilized sources to examine its subject. The alternative black curriculum found its expression in a variety of concrete pedagogical forms, including plays, pageants, and textbooks. The utility of these sources is often not understood by current scholars because these alternative sources are frequently viewed as less credible than literature or scholarly work within university settings. I contend that these materials, created by black women during this period, are worth being studied based on their own merits. The pedagogical choices of African American women had a major impact on the construction of knowledge in social studies. Because these women operated outside of traditional university settings and through alternative means of communication, educators and historians may have been slow to recognize the construction of the alternative black curriculum. These *historians without a portfolio* deserve to have their work be at the center of the discussion in a number of different academic disciplines.[6] This book examines the impact of these women in shaping the development of the alternative black curriculum through plays, pageants, and textbooks that reflect a coherent ideological identity that profoundly shaped the current K-12 social studies curriculum.

This book has three thematic goals. First, this book is deliberately intersectional by drawing on the fields of education history and social studies through a focus on the efforts of African American women at the secondary school level to develop the alternative black curriculum. I will argue that the alternative black curriculum demonstrates how black women scholars and

---

[5] LaGarrett J. King, Ryan Crowley, and Anthony L. Brown, "The Forgotten Legacy of Carter G. Woodson: Contributions to Multicultural Social Studies and African-American History," *The Social Studies* 101 (2010): 211–215.

[6] Pero Gaglo Dagbovie, *African American History Reconsidered* (Urbana: University of Illinois Press, 2010), 103.

educators offered a theoretical and practical critique of the more prominent education reform movements in the United States.[7] Second, this book offers the first comprehensive account of how black women scholars impacted the development of the social studies curriculum. Important scholarly work by Sarah Bair, Julie Des Jardins, LaGarrett King, and Pero Gaglo Dagbovie has addressed the efforts of individual black women in this area, yet this book is the first to examine the discursive work of black women educators on the content and the pedagogy of social studies as it related to black children. Finally, this book offers an important examination of how current school reform can incorporate the lessons learned from the alternative black curriculum.

THE ALTERNATIVE BLACK CURRICULUM IN SOCIAL STUDIES

The Progressive Era is increasingly being viewed as a foundational period in educational history. Likewise, my work is informed by existing scholarship on black education during the period of 1890–1940. Recent scholarship has emphasized how major black intellectuals focused on educational theory in their work. For instance, Derrick P. Aldridge created an educational history of W.E.B. Du Bois's educational philosophy and contributions to the field of education. Aldridge used case studies of African American leaders to demonstrate how Progressive Era educators engaged in a dialogue about how to teach black children. Notable, however, is a distinctly masculine bias present in the increased focus on the black educators of the Progressive Era. For example, the representative debate between Booker T. Washington and W.E.B. Du Bois often dominates the relevant literature. Similarly, the work of Carter G. Woodson is often cited by scholars who do extend their work. Jeffrey Aaron Snyder persuasively outlined that the basic tenets of Carter G. Woodson's critique of black education can be squarely placed at the center of a Progressive tradition. Snyder contended that *The Mis-Education of the Negro* connects deeply with a major claim of Progressive educators, that education must be relevant to students' lives and interests.[8]

A limited but growing set of educational histories have attempted to correct this masculine bias within relevant educational literature. Margaret

---

[7] Derrick P. Aldridge, *The Educational Thought of W.E.B. Du Bois: An Intellectual History* (New York: Teachers College Press, 2006).

[8] Jeffrey A. Snyder, "Progressive Education in Black and White: Rereading Carter G. Woodson's *Mis-Education of the Negro*," *History of Education Quarterly* 55, no. 3 (August 2015): 273–293.

Nash and Sarah Bair explored the educational values of Nannie H. Burroughs, Anna Julia Cooper, and Mary Church Terrell. Julie Des Jardins examined how black women educators contributed to the development of histories in the United States.[9] Christine Woyshner presented an examination of the impact and extensive network of black women's civic organizations on educational outcomes.[10] More recently, LaGarrett King examined black history textbooks written by Merle Eppes, Edward A. Johnson, and Leila Amos Pendleton, deconstructing how these scholars expanded definitions of citizenship from 1890 to 1940. Each of these previous scholars links black women to Progressive Era education reform.

Although black women's intellectual theory did not receive the same manner of public attention as Du Bois, Washington, and Woodson, the collective nature of their work speaks to how black women persistently created, implemented, and applied Progressive principles to their work as educators.

The latter half of the time period studied spans the Harlem Renaissance and World War II. The Harlem Renaissance is particularly important because it is during this period the focus on black history as seen in the individual works of Leila Amos Pendleton, Carter G. Woodson, Laura Eliza Wilkes, and W.E.B. Du Bois becomes more collective and widespread. The emergence of the *Negro History Bulletin* and *The Brownies' Book* and the formation of the International Council of the Women of the Darker Races (ICWDR) demonstrated the growing ranks of educators disseminating black history. The second half of this book will consider this period during the development of the alternative black curriculum.

Drawing on the work of educational historians, I specifically focus on the work of black educators in one specific environment, the K-12 classroom. This offers real insight into the contributions of black women to educational theory. The story of K-12 education development is enriched if we examine how black women historians constructed knowledge at the beginning of the twentieth century. The schools created during

---

[9] Sarah Bair, "Educating Black Girls in the Early 20th Century: The Pioneering Work of Nannie Helen Burroughs: (1879–1961)," *Theory and Research in Social Education* 36 (Winter 2008): 9–35. Julie Ellyn Des Jardins, "Reclaiming the Past and Present: Women, Gender and the Construction of Historical Memory in America, 1880–1940," (PhD diss., Brown University, 2000), 270. Margaret A. Nash, "Patient Persistence: The Political and Educational Values of Anna Julia Cooper and Mary Church Terrell." *Educational Studies* 35 (April 2004): 122–136.

[10] Christine Woyshner, *The National Parent Teacher Association, Race and Civil Engagement, 1897–1970*. (Columbus, Ohio: 2009).

Reconstruction provided an opportunity for black women to create curriculum which challenged racism. The alternative black curriculum demonstrates how black scholars critiqued more prominent education reform movements in the United States. In undergraduate and graduate social studies seminars across the nation, the typical narrative of how the social studies field developed reads:

> The NEA Committee of Ten (1892) under the leadership of Charles William Eliot created a standardized curriculum, which is still in use in secondary schools in the twenty first century. In these meetings these esteemed men suggested a course of study which included world history, US history and government. This course of study has been taught in American schools for over 100 years.

This book, however, contributes to a new and more complete narrative in the historiography of the field of social studies. A more complete narrative of the formation of the social studies field would include the following statement:

> Beginning in the early twentieth century, a group of black intellectuals, inclusive of men and women, drawing on the knowledge of early historical writings began to shape a narrative of the African American experience in the United States. This significant educational reform institutionalized the black history movement which is present in schools today. Along with white groups such as the Committee of Ten, it altered how students learn social studies in the twentieth century.

Educational historians are constantly working to make the context of history relevant to the work of modern schools. The collective amnesia demonstrated by school reformers constantly frustrates historians who seek to demonstrate the consistency of patterns which undermine school improvement attempts.

This book concludes that two important lessons that have implications for the study of schools today can be learned by understanding the history of the alternative black curriculum: intellectual hybridity and creation of knowledge.

The authors of the alternative black curriculum exhibited an intellectual hybridity, which I argue is a key character trait of successful multicultural educators. This intellectual hybridity surfaced in multiple ways. First, these educators worked diligently at using scholarly knowledge to inform curricular creation. Secondly, they used knowledge to move critical issues to the black community forward. Finally, their work linked the activities of the broader community with the landscape of the school. This book presents a comprehensive case that modern teachers must begin to exhibit this characteristic of the black women educators to create a richer intellectual environment for all students, instead of relying on prescribed curriculums and system level dictates.

The understanding of the creation of knowledge is important in reshaping the debate of public schools today. For example, under the strictures of No Child Left Behind and the Race to the Top grants, the school curriculum—social studies, in particular—weathered constant attacks on the intellectualism which grounds meaningful historical work. Teachers were viewed as vessels to promote test-taking strategies, and their creative role as innovators was reduced. The development of the alternative black curriculum will present educators who struggled against state and local control by creating pageants, lesson plans, articles, and work groups that promoted a more complex understanding of US and world history.

Through the lens of the alternative black curriculum, I will make the argument that teachers must not only enact the curriculum, they must actively create materials that constantly challenge a dominant narrative in the social studies. By understanding the substantial dialogue between black women during the period from 1890 to 1940 about how black children should be taught about their history, we can contextualize how a respectful academic discourse can improve outcomes for our nation's neediest children. Reform, in this instance, means recovery.

The Organization of Countering the Master Narrative

This book is organized in a series of case studies, refining the historical methods generally applied to study black women which typically employ a biographical approach to their lives. While the biographical approach is useful for establishing a chronology, it should be supplemented in a way that investigates the works of these educators with a sharper eye to the curriculum choices they made as they taught and led schools in the black community. Moreover, a challenge in crafting a simple biographical narrative is that the sources associated with the lives of black women educators are fragmented and leave no consistent "paper trail." As Jill Lepore notes in the *Book of Ages: The Life and Opinions of Jane Franklin*:

> In writing this book I have had to stare down a truism: the lives of the obscure make good fiction but bad history. For an eighteenth-century woman of her rank and station, Jane Franklin Mecom's life is exceptionally well documented, but, by any other measure, her paper trail is miserably scant. (Lepore 2013)

By contrast, a case study method looks to explore the nuances of each educator's contributions while also exploring how the educators' "web of affiliations" allowed for fruitful conversations between authors and their colleagues. Using a case study method to write about the contributions of black women allows us to build a group picture of their collective impact on the social studies curriculum. Moreover, these black women educators often wrote in public sources; the sources associated with their private lives are not as consistent. For instance, Laura E. Eliza Wilkes, the author of *Missing Pages in American History: Revealing the Services of Negroes in the Early Wars of the United States, 1641–1815*, left few details about her life. When she is referenced in a speech by prominent black politician, John Edward Bruce, we get a small glimpse into her impact on the black community. Her story demonstrates the difficulty in collecting consistent sources on an individual level. A case study method can create a mosaic of smaller stories that adds to understanding the group effects of the drafting of curriculum.

Chapter 2 will present a case study of the social studies curriculum of the National Training School for Women and Girls. Nannie H. Burroughs's leadership style will be discussed in analyzing her attempt to implement a black history curriculum at her school. Primary source documents from the Nannie H. Burroughs archives located at the Library of Congress will be reviewed, as well as curriculum documents such as lesson plans, black history month agendas, and student work to analyze Burroughs's effectiveness in shaping the social studies curricula in her building.

Chapter 3 will consider the crucial impact of pageants, which presented two broad themes of the alternative black curriculum to the larger public. First, pageants were experimental sites because ideas central to the development of the alternative black curriculum were tested. Second, pageants were written expressions of the alternative black curriculum. These themes will be explored by considering five key pageants written during this period: *The Star of Ethiopia* (1915) by W.E.B. Dubois, *When Truth Gets a Hearing* (1919) by Nannie H. Burroughs, *Out of the Dark* (1924) by Dorothy C. Guinn, *Two Races* (1930) by Inez Burke, and *The Light of the Women* (1930) by Frances Gunner.

Chapter 4 will examine the process of "narrative rewriting" of a counter-canon as an essential part of the development of the alternative black curriculum. First, the chapter will consider the different institutional visions of Carter G. Woodson and W.E.B. Du Bois as they sought to define the contours of the alternative black curriculum. I will consider the impact of periodicals on the development of the alternative black curriculum in social studies. Two periodicals will be presented: *The Brownies' Book* and *The Negro History Bulletin*. Edited by W.E.B. Dubois and Jessie Redmon Fauset, *The Brownies' Book* was the first literary magazine targeting African American children and used history and literature as way to inspire the readers into political action. *The Negro History Bulletin,* edited by a variety of editors, was directed toward teachers. I will then examine the career of Leila Amos Pendleton who wrote *A Narrative of the Negro* (1912), one of the few textbooks written by black women during the Progressive Era. Included in this chapter will be a textual analysis of *A Narrative of the Negro* emphasizing the major themes in the alternative black curriculum in social studies. In addition, I will compare the texts, *Unsung Heroes* by Elizabeth Ross Haynes and *Missing Pages in American History* by Laura Eliza Wilkes as exemplars of books which also challenge narratives in textbooks. Finally, the chapter will examine the books *The Mis-Education of the Negro* (1933) and *Black Reconstruction* (1935) as examples of the counter-canon that are embodied in the alternative black curriculum.

Chapter 5 will survey the literature on teaching training and its impact of the development of the alternative black curriculum in social studies. This chapter explores the different modes of training teachers to teach history in segregated schools. Unlike in previous chapters, this chapter will focus primarily on black male educators such as Booker T. Washington, W.E.B. Du Bois, Reid T. Jackson, and Ambrose Caliver. Of the policy making spaces considered in this book, the discussions in higher education demonstrated the least openness to the ideas of black female educators. The chapter will add dimension to the work of Booker T. Washington in his argument of black teacher training in the twentieth century.

Chapter 6 will consider the intersection of the alternative black curriculum and policy advocacy during the early twentieth century. I will discuss the organizational history of the International Council of Women of the Darker Races, established in 1922 by a group of prominent black women activists. Then, the introduction of dialogical spaces as a conceptual framework to illuminate the work of the ICWDR at the intersection of the alternative black curriculum and policy advocacy will be analyzed in three ways: first, by how the educational agenda of the ICWDR, which consisted of educating the black community about contemporary and historical events in the African diaspora, intersected with its larger policy goals; second, through a description of the type of materials that ICWDR promoted and disseminated in black history and social studies to achieve its policy goals; and finally, by how the country of Haiti played a particularly important role in the advocacy work of the women activists of the ICWDR. This chapter extends the themes of the book by tracing an intellectual history of black women activists during the time period.

The Conclusion will consider how the impact of the alternative black curriculum still reverberates in the Post-Brown education landscape. In the concluding chapter, I will make the argument that utilizing the social construct of race is essential to future studies in social studies field. Finally, I will discuss how understanding the contributions of black women practitioners to scholarly discourse will improve instructional practices and pedagogy in our nation's public schools.

CHAPTER 2

Moving Beyond Biography: Critical Race Theory and the Construction of the Alternative Black Curriculum in Social Studies

Beginning in the mid-1920s, the National Training School for Women and Girls in Washington DC hosted an annual Appreciation Day, a practice that started during the 1920s. Its program, dated 1929, contained a quote attributed to its founder and president, Nannie Helen Burroughs, "to pay tribute to those men and women who worked for abolition of slavery and those who helped establish the 'going' of race in America."[1] This quote captures the central purpose of these programs—the inspirational celebration of the history of African Americans in the United States through music, oratory, poems, and prayers.

At the fifth annual Appreciation Day, Miss Doris Nelson, a student, recited a speech about the Underground Railroad and another student, Miss Georgiana Butler, spoke on the "Appreciation of the Negroes' African Background." These speeches typified the oration that occurred on Appreciation Days, namely, aiding students' comprehension of Nannie H. Burroughs's vision of African American history. A sign of Burroughs's historical vision stands out on this program—something, which on the surface may seem a little thing. That in a world which often devalued young African American women, both young women were referred to as "Miss." Burroughs constructed a vision of a school grounded in a black history narrative that would instill a sense of pride for the Black girls at NTS (Fig. 2.1).

[1] Burroughs, *Appreciation Day Program*, Box 312, Library of Congress. The word "going" is in the program; it means the continuing struggle of African Americans.

© The Author(s) 2018
A. D. Murray, *The Development of the Alternative Black Curriculum, 1890–1940,*
https://doi.org/10.1007/978-3-319-91418-3_2

1926   1930

FOURTH ANNUAL
"APPRECIATION DAY"
originated and observed by the

The National Training School for Women and Girls, Inc.

MISS NANNIE H. BURROUGHS, President

1930 PROGRAM

FEBRUARY 23, 3:30 P.M.

Music "America The Beautiful"..........(Standing) School and Audience
Scripture..
Prayer (Standing)...
Chant...
Music "Listen to the Lambs"—Dett..........Training School Choral Club
Oration—"They Found a Way—On the Underground Railroad".................
                                                         Miss Eleanor Morton, Mass.
Music—Solo—"Wade in de Water"—Burleigh........Miss E. B. Riley, Ga.
Oration—"John Brown"......................Miss Gertrude Hewitt, N.Y.
Music—"Battle Hymn of the Republic" with Chorus of "John Brown's Body"...School and Audience
Oration—"Seven Great Workers in the Cause of Freedom"..................
                                                               Miss Helen King, Pa.
Music—"Deep River"—Burleigh..............Training School Choral Club
Oration—Lincoln's Gettysburg Speech"......Miss Gaynelle Horne, Conn.
Music—"America".....................................School and Audience
Oration—"What White Americans Have Done to Aid the Negro in His Upward Climb"............................Miss Alma Roberts, Ga.
Music—"Lift Every Voice and Sing"—Johnson......School and Audience
Oration—"How the Two Races Can Work Together to Build A Christian Civilization"..............................Miss Alice Smith, N.Y.
Music {(a) "Come All of God's Children", arranged by Work..............
      {(b) "Music in the Mine", Dett......Training School Choral Club

---

Please help the School. We have a deficit of FIVE THOUSAND DOLLARS. Will you make a contribution? When? The need is pressing.

Hear Honorable Oscar DePriest at the Training School Mass Meeting at the Metropolitan A. M. E. Church, M Street, between 15th and 16th Streets, Northwest, March 7th.

See the Training School girls in their beautiful pageant—"When Truth Gets a Hearing"—Armstrong High School Auditorium, March 27th.

Fig. 2.1 Fourth Annual Appreciation Day. (Nannie H. Burroughs, Papers of Nannie H. Burroughs, Library of Congress *Appreciation Day Program,* Box 312)

FIFTH ANNUAL
APPRECIATION DAY

Set apart and observed

on the 22nd Day of February

by the

THE NATIONAL TRAINING SCHOOL FOR WOMEN AND GIRLS, Inc.

Nannie H. Burroughs, President

To pay tribute to those men and women who worked for the abolition of slavery, and those who helped to establish the "going" of our race in America.

REMEMBER

That by the emancipation act "Abraham Lincoln made merely a race possibility. Only the Negro himself can make this possibility real."

MUSICAL PROLOGUE

1. "Invictus"—Huhn   Glee Club
2. Solo "Ole Man River"—Kern - Miss Eula Bell Riley, Ga.
3. Solo "Water Boy"—Robinson. - Miss Ruth Gibbs, N.Y.

PROGRAM

1. Music "My Country 'Tis of Thee" - School and Audience
2. Prayer
3. Music "Your Land and My Land"—Shubert - Glee Club
4. Introductory "The Meaning of Appreciation Day",
   Miss Ruth Gibbs
5. "America The Beautiful"   School and Audience
6. Oration "Appreciation of the Negro's African Background" - Miss Georgiana Parks, Africa, 1st Yr.
7. Oration "Toussaint L'Overture",—Wendell Phillips
   Miss L. Spellman, Conn, 4th Yr
8. Music "We've Fought Every Race's Battle"—Burroughs
   Glee Club
9. Oration "The Underground Railroad and Its Conductors"
   Miss Doris Nelson, N.Y., 2nd Yr.
10. Music "Hymn of Freedom"—Burlin   Glee Club
11. Oration "John Brown", Miss Helen Jones, N.Y., Jr. High
12. Poem "John Brown of Ossawatomie" Miss Ethel Wallace, N.Y., Jr. High
13. Music "Battle Hymn of the Republic" School & Audience
14. Oration "Women Workers in the Cause of Freedom"
    Miss Alice Smith, N.Y., 3rd Yr.
15. Oration "Mightier than the Sword" - Miss Jessie Williams
    Michigan, Jr. College
16. Music "Soldiers' Chorus" — Gounod (From the opera "Faust") Glee Club
17. Oration "Educating the Negro to make His Emancipation Real," Miss Helen King, Pa., 4th Yr.
18. Oration "As America Goes Marching On"
    Miss Hazel Barnes, Pa., 2nd Yr.
19. Music, National Negro Anthem, "Lift Every Voice and Sing"—Johnson   Glee Club

PRIZES:—First and second prizes will be awarded class representatives—PLEASE VOTE.

REFRESHMENTS WILL BE SERVED
IN THE TRADES HALL

Reproduced from the Collections of the Manuscript Division, Library of Congress

Fig. 2.1 (continued)

FREEDOM AND JUSTICE FOREVER
SIXTH ANNUAL
APPRECIATION DAY
Set apart and observed

on the Twenty-second Day of February
at the
THE NATIONAL TRAINING SCHOOL FOR WOMEN AND GIRLS, Inc.
Nannie H. Burroughs, President

To pay tribute to the men and women who worked for the abolition of slavery and those who helped establish the "going" of our race in America.

REMEMBER
The Emancipation act "made merely a race possibility. Only the Negro himself can make this possibility real."

PROGRAM

Music (all standing)—"Star-Spangled Banner" ....
Prayer .... Miss Denniston
Scripture—Joshua 4: 1-9. .... Mrs. Etta Versa Frye
A Statement—"Why Appreciation Day" ....
                              Miss Estelle Johnson, New Jersey
Music—"Land of Hope and Glory"—Elgan ..... Choral Society
Oration—"Africa, The American Negro's Background" ......
                              Miss Georgeanna Parks, Africa
Reading—"Out of the Wilderness"... Miss Harriet Harris, Pa.
Music—Spiritual "Don't Be A Weary Traveler"—Dett ......
Oration—"Frederick Douglass" ..... Miss Ethel Millner, N. Y.
Oration—"They Found A Way Out of Slavery—Over The Underground Railroad" .... Miss Elizabeth Jones, Wis.
Music—"Speed the Republic."—Keller ....
Oration—"Lincoln's Supreme Purpose" .... Miss Lois Orr, Ill.
Reading—"The Colored Soldiers" .... Miss Ada Williams, N.Y.
Music—"The New Hail Columbia,"—Chadwick ....
Oration—"The Spirit of Lincoln" ..... Miss Helen Jones. N.Y.
Music (all) "Battle Hymn of the Republic" ....
Oration—"What Price, O Freedom" .... Miss Alice Smith, N.Y.
Music—Spirituals—(a) "Lord What a Morning"—Burleigh.
        (b) "Peter Go Ring Them Bells" ....
Oration—"Our Second Emancipation"... Miss Jessie Williams, Michigan
Music—"Lift Every Voice And Sing" (Negro National Anthem)—Johnson

---

PLEASE—Vote for the best orators of the day.

HAVE DINNER (at Burdette Home) PRICE FIFTY CENTS

Help us in our Drive, March 7–April 17. You can form a group of ten and raise One Hundred Dollars.
Congressman Oscar DePriest, Chairman Citizen's Committee
THANK YOU

The Best way to express our appreciation for what has been done for us is to do more for ourselves.

Fig. 2.1 (continued)

Yet, the program served as more than uplift for its students. The annual Appreciation Days served as a crucial fundraising tool, which was necessary for the independent school's continued survival. Equally important was that the annual Appreciation Days at NTS imparted a specific narrative about the history of the United States. One that demonstrated black educators' attempts to reframe national and international educational curriculum to include an accurate re-telling of the struggle of African Americans during the Progressive Era.[2] I refer to this counter-narrative as the *alternative black curriculum* throughout the remainder of this book. The alternative black curriculum comprises both the content and pedagogy and space where these educators implemented the curriculum.

A study of the alternative black curriculum is necessary considering our changing understanding of how the development of social studies curriculum occurred in the early twentieth century. The alternative black curriculum draws on a few key insights. The first draws on the work of Pero Gaglo Dagbovie, Anthony Brown, and Jeffrey Aaron Snyder who all argue that increased attention needs to be paid to the construction of an alternative historical narrative in the field of social studies. These scholars posit that during the period 1890–1940, African American scholars created divergent discourses in social studies, with Carter G. Woodson's sustained promotion of black history receiving the most attention. Recently, Anthony Brown, Ryan Crowley, and LaGarrett King explored how Carter G. Woodson's textbook created an alternative narrative in the social studies about the role of African American men in the military.[3]

This work in educational scholarship is supplemented by the work of historians such as Stephen G. Hall who sought to explore how African American scholars, historians, clergy, and abolitionists developed an alternative narrative to the dominant narrative of history created by white scholars. Hall, in particular, argued that black historical writers challenged the dominant narrative by emphasizing that while in the nineteenth century, these texts were being produced despite the lack of formal training of their authors. The advent of the twentieth century brought a new crop of university-trained black male scholars as well as a wider dissemination

---

[2] Des Jardins, *Reclaiming the Past and Present*, 265.
[3] Anthony L. Brown, Ryan M. Crowley, and LaGarrett J. King, "Black Civitas: An Examination of Carter G. Woodson's Contributions to Teaching About Race, Citizenship, and the Black Soldier," *Theory and Research in Social Education* 39, no.2 (Spring 2011): 278–299.

of earlier works by black scholars. Consequently, by the early twentieth century a professional class of historians emerged that was devoted to reshaping narratives about the African American historical experience in the United States.[4]

Historically, scholars have used terms such as *historical memory* or the *black history narrative* to describe these developments. These references have almost been an exclusive one of male scholars in university settings. Pero Gaglo Dagbovie remains the outlier having also studied the role of women in the Association of Negro Life and History. Most of the scholarship around the formation the alternative black curriculum tends to focus on men. My reference to its construction captures an intersectional focus on gender and praxis in its creation. I argue that black women educational reformers served in a coequal relationship with males in the development of a new social studies narrative, through the engagement of theoretical content with specific practical technique.

Burroughs's visionary application of the principles of the alternative black curriculum are among the examples of educators who produced the frameworks, texts, courses, historical pageants, speeches, and curriculum materials used in community, church, and school settings to nurture the development of African American children. The choices she made are fascinating examples of how a school leader created a theory of action to challenge dominant narratives. Burroughs represents a pivotal case of an educator who dealt with one of the central challenges women reformers in the social studies confronted as she attempted to combine "low-status practice" with efforts to create new epistemologies.[5]

The second scholarly insight the alternative black curriculum draws from comes from critical race theory. Critical race theory (CRT) emerged in academia in the 1980s and 1990s when theorists such as Derrick Bell, Richard Delgado, and Kimberlé Crenshaw articulated a specific set of jurisprudential principles to guide scholars in analyzing how minorities experience the legal system in the United States. Out of incredibly complex literature, the three basic premises emerged within critical race theory: (1) the claim on the proposition that "racism is

---

[4] Stephen G. Hall. *A Faithful Account of the Race: African American Historical Writing in Nineteenth Century America*. Chapel Hill: The University of North Carolina Press, 2009.

[5] Christine Woyshner, "Notes towards a Historiography of Social Studies," in *Research Methods in Social Studies Education: Contemporary Issues and Perspectives* ed., Keith Barton (Greenwich, CT: Information Age Publishing, 2006), 3.

normal, not aberrant in American society," (2) the claim that focuses on the creation of "counter-narratives," and (3) the claim that focuses on the concept of "interest convergence," which states that social reform only occurs when demands for change by minority groups align with the interests of elites.[6] The application of critical race theory has been extended to educational theory.

The emergence of the alternative black curriculum in social studies brings attention to the prevalence of race as a construct in a generation of new epistemologies in social studies. The work of Gloria Ladson-Billings plays an influential role in asserting that the theoretical framework of CRT applies to questions of equality in education. She argued that "[i]f we look at the way that public education is currently configured, it is possible to see that CRT can be a powerful experience for the sustained inquiry into what people of color experience."[7] Ladson-Billings further noted that a CRT perspective is useful in framing questions in social studies research as it addresses the silences about race and racism in the curriculum. For example, researchers tend to ignore or minimize race in examining how students approach understanding primary source documents. Critical race theory supports the idea that the formation of a student's racial identity is a critical component in how students learn in different subject areas, including social studies. To reframe the question with a focus on race, a CRT researcher might ask, "[h]ow might a student's race affect the knowledge and the schema he brings to the document?" In Tyrone Howard and Terrie Epstein's research, the use of the race lens demonstrates new directions that infuse added complexity into research on the social studies which need to be embraced by emerging educational researchers.

CRT has direct applications in education history in two ways beyond its impact on reframing an underlying research methodology in its educational theory. First, critical race theorists have offered materials examinations that consider previously suppressed viewpoints—a reconstructive purpose. Educational historians' work is reconstructive in nature, so it was not challenging to incorporate CRT into my work. Critical race theory illuminates how the social construct of race impacted the public pedagogy of African American educators. A second direct application of CRT

---

[6] Derrick Bell, "*Brown v. Board of Education* and the interest convergence dilemma," *Harvard Law Review* 93: (Jan. 1980): 518–533.

[7] Gloria Ladson-Billings, "Just what is Critical Race Theory and what is it doing in a nice field like education?" *Qualitative Studies in Education* 11 (1998): 7–24.

in education emerged from the work of Kimberlé Crenshaw.[8] Crenshaw's intersectional framework informed the development of Burroughs's leadership of NTS as a case study of a woman negotiating power dynamics of her race, class, and gender in leading an independent private boarding school aimed at training working class girls for citizenship in a democracy.

Unlike many public black school principals under segregation, Burroughs could operate her building without oversight from white school boards.[9] Her relative freedom enabled her to offer a more varied curriculum and provided her with the liberty to go about the "practical" work of her school with a creative flair. She worked to infuse her narratives about black history into the rich complexities of school life, and authored a portion of the alternative black curriculum in her pageant, *When Truth Gets a Hearing*. Ironically, Burroughs was afforded the opportunity that Carter G. Woodson and W.E.B. Du Bois never had or desired as intellectual academics—the ability to operationalize an alternative black curriculum in social studies for a school.

A number of studies have addressed Nannie Helen Burroughs's attempts to engage in the construction of an alternative black curriculum, yet this work has typically utilized a biographical approach. I believe that an analytical framework exists that can help us to comprehend the sophisticated strategies utilized to embody historical memory in a comprehensive educational setting.

Methodological Considerations

The typical historical construction of the contributions of the "founding mothers" of black women history is a biographical sketch approach. In constructing this paper, however, I refined the approach to defining the work of black women educators. As I set to study Nannie H. Burroughs's leadership, my methodological focus sought to provide context for the work of her instructional leadership. In redefining the contours of the field of education historians, I would argue that historians should provide biographies about the female talented tenth but also investigate the work of

---

[8] Kimberlé Crenshaw, "Mapping the Margins: Intersectionality, Identity Politics, and Violence Against Women of Color," *Stanford Law Review* 43, no. 6 (July 1991): 1241–1299.
[9] Vanessa Siddle Walker, *Hello Professor: a black principal and professional leadership in the segregated south* (Chapel Hill, NC: University of North Carolina Press, 2009).

these educators with a sharper eye to the curriculum choices they made as they taught and led schools in the black community.

Historians note that researching change in instructional practices over time is challenging.[10] Unlike contemporary qualitative researchers who can capture conversations between individuals via digital means, the historian's analysis of dialogue which occurred between administrators and staff is limited to extant archival records. Nonetheless, faculty meeting notes from Burroughs's staff meetings developed as rich sources for understanding the evolution of her social studies curriculum. In those meetings she gave motivational speeches, set clear expectations for students, and focused on the daily logistics of operating the school. And her teachers gave updates about the performances of students and expressed frustrations about classroom management. These documents provided insight into the dialogue that informed the social studies curriculum in the NTS building.

To develop a curriculum history at NTS, I explored documents that gave voices to the teachers in the building—lesson plans. Lesson plans served a foundational role in my analysis of teacher work. They are particularly important in recapturing teachers' daily instructional decisions. A survey of the lesson plans also demonstrated how teachers reconciled Burroughs's vision with the insistent demands of classroom instruction.

I also searched for student voice in constructing this curriculum history. Capturing student voice, recovering their thoughts and ideas, proves challenging for the education historian because students often had the least amount of power in a school setting. In order for me to capture the faint sound of student voices, I surveyed documents that showed how students participated in the school. The Appreciation Day programs provided information about when students conducted speeches, and the *1929 Student Annual* is where students summarized key events that happened during the school year. Additionally, I analyzed answers on students' history examinations and also considered two student projects, one on Dorie Miller, the first African American sailor to receive the Navy Cross, and the other on the history of Germany during World War II. Both provided insight into the knowledge students were accruing in their history classes.

---

[10] Larry Cuban, *How Teachers Taught: Constancy and Change in American Classrooms 1890–1990* (New York: Teacher College Press, 1994).

Teaching and Learning at NTS

Nannie H. Burroughs attempted to create discourses that challenged the inferiority paradigm about African American children. She met with varying degrees of success in her achievement of that vision. One of the distinct roles of a school's principal is to create a school culture that embraces the needs of the students. In the book, *Young Gifted and Black*, Theresa Perry articulated a theory of academic achievement for African American children. She argued that African American schools were "intentionally organized to oppose the ideology of Black intellectual inferiority."[11] Burroughs attempted to create a school that tried to resist the dominant culture's attempts to categorize African American children as inferior. In constructing NTS, she created curriculum, clubs, and activities which, in Perry's words, attempted to affirm her students' "Black humanity, Black intelligence, and Black achievement."[12]

Nannie Helen Burroughs succeeded in creating a whole school culture that socialized African American girls to assume leadership roles in the larger society. The constant emphasis on exuding positive and respectful messages for students in their interactions with staff and the continual emphasis on the black women historical figures created an environment that nurtured the girls' growth and development. Her creation of a separate gendered space is unique, as she was able to reinterpret the dominant historical narrative to fit the needs of the underserved identity of the black female. Yet, despite her success in shaping the larger school culture, Burroughs experienced less success in shaping the instruction of the individual classroom teacher. The tension between principals and their ability to control the curriculum of classroom teachers is a continual theme in educational research.

Nannie H. Burroughs created NTS to support the development of African American girls. She emphasized the importance virtue and advocated for a space for black girls to develop an identity centered on Christian service to the community and success.[13] The NTS social studies program was developed with those purposes in mind. Her belief in the necessity of education for African American girls is illustrated in one of her promotional brochures:

---

[11] Perry, *Young, Gifted and Black*, 88.
[12] Ibid.
[13] Burroughs, *Miss Burroughs Appeals to Parents to Save Their Girls Now*, undated, Box 46.

Our race will be morally bankrupt if parents do not put first things first in the care and protection of their daughters. If they must be away from home all day, they should send their daughters to the best Christian boarding schools, so that they can get the kind of training that will prepare them for the great day of economic competition that is surely coming.[14]

Although Burroughs appealed to parents' sense of morality and race loyalty as a means to enroll more students, the young women were exposed to a more radical environment. She generated a space where African American girls could see themselves and their contributions to history at the center of the curriculum and developed a school that combated the patriarchy of the black community.

Nannie Helen Burroughs articulated a clear set of principles to guide instruction at NTS. At the heart of her instructional vision was her desire for her staff to learn about the lives and interests of the girls attending the school. She encouraged her staff to "get to know the girls in order to motivate them."[15] She exhorted her staff to exhibit a high level of enthusiasm in working with the students during and after school. In a rousing speech to NTS faculty on November 22, 1942, Burroughs stated:

> We have gone through difficult days here, but I am convinced that God is going to restore us very fully all of the things we have had and that He is going to give us more things. I believe that God is helping me by giving those who take this work as seriously as I do.......
>
> "A CAUSE LIKE THIS" requires that we-
>
> 1. Know Young People.
> 2. Influence in character ideals
>
> It requires "heart interest" in our ideal.
> "A CAUSE LIKE THIS" means team-work.
> "A CAUSE LIKE THIS" is hurt, damaged, destroyed, and defeated by petty, selfish, weak, lazy teachers.[16]

Burroughs expected an immense amount of passion for students being educated in her building, and this speech demonstrated the level of passion Burroughs brought to her work as leader of the school.

[14] Burroughs, *Miss Burroughs Appeals to Parents to Save Their Girls Now*, undated, Box 46.
[15] Burroughs, *Faculty Meeting Notes,* November 22, 1942, Box 46.
[16] Burroughs, *Faculty Meeting Notes,* Box 46.

Burroughs viewed education as an ethical enterprise wherein teachers served as important role models for the girls in the building. Her expectations were detailed in the NTS *Code of Professional Ethics*. In the document, Burroughs encouraged her teachers to "dignify their calling" in their interaction with students. She encouraged staff not to critique their supervisors and cooperate with the administration of the building, emphasizing that teachers be kind and refrain from gossip about co-workers. She ended the document with the phrase, "A word fitly spoken is like apples of gold in pitchers of silver."[17]

In a humorous little survey, Burroughs queried the professional attitude of her staff, asking questions such as: "Do you have a good alibi for your mistakes? Do you often wear a martyr's expression? Do you denounce every set of new pupils as "dumber than the last"? Do you say Yes, but this is different- in reference to your shortcomings? Do you beat the children to the door at dismissal?"[18] Although the survey employed a sarcastic tone, Burroughs sought to show teachers that having high standards and love for your work was fundamental to being a staff member at her school (Fig. 2.2).

An undated document I reviewed outlined Burroughs's principles of a successful classroom. She encouraged teachers to provide a well-organized classroom that supported student learning. Burroughs advocated for drills and a series of higher order thinking questions to convey critical facts to students. She supported instruction with a daily planning period. She suggested that teachers use the radio to learn about key events in the community. She advocated for debates to execute student learning. She encouraged students to tutor other students. Compared to descriptions of traditional education in early twentieth century, Burroughs exuded a slightly modern sensibility about how staff should interact with the student population. In an era where conservative instruction methods were the norm, Burroughs supported a variety of methods that encouraged students' participation and excitement. She sought to create a school where students were engaged in a student-centered learning environment.[19]

Although Burroughs appeared to be quite strict with her expectations, her staff was afforded the opportunity to be respectful participants in building her vision through voicing their opinions and concerns. This is illustrated

[17] Burroughs, *Code of Professional Ethics*, undated, Box 311.
[18] Burroughs, *Take Your Professional Temperature*, undated, Box 311.
[19] Burroughs, *Take Your Professional Temperature*, undated, Box 311.

TAKE YOUR PROFESSIONAL TEMPERATURE.

1. Do you have a good alibi for your mistakes?
2. Do you say "Yes, but this is different," in reference to your shortcomings?
3. Do you often complain of overwork?
4. Do you wear a martyr's expression?
5. Do you often get to work two or three minutes late?
6. Do you denounce every new set of pupils as "dumber" than the last?
7. Do you beat the children to the door at dismissal?
8. Do you sit in on committee and faculty meetings with an I'd - rather be - anywhere - than - here air?
9. Do you watch the clock every time you attend a meeting?
10. Do you discuss other teachers with the pupils?
11. Do you belittle the efforts of those who do more than you?
12. Do you keep silent and thereby give approval when your school and your superiors are criticised in your presence?
13. Do you repeat school gossip in such a way as to let ordinary unflattering incidents assume serious proportions?
14. Do you think teachers are overly imposed upon?
15. Do you think you have more to do than anyone else?
16. Do you declaim bitterly when any extra work looms?
17. Do you shudder at the thought of being observed?
18. Do you go to class without an idea of what you're going to do?
19. Do you berate your pupils for doing the same thing?
20. Do you disapprove of argument in the classroom?
21. Do you disregard general untidiness in the room?
22. Is your bulletin board blank? Cluttered? Stale?
23. Do you yearn loudly for Fridays?
24. Do you have to hunt for your supplies?
25. Are you amused to relate the stories of private home life of children who naively tell you of their skeletons in the closet?
26. Do you turn a deaf ear to pupil's personal problems and confidences?
27. Do you impale a pupil with a quick stab of sarcasm?
28. Do you shout to gain attention?
29. Do children find you hard to approach?
30. Do you ever get around looking inside of a Journal of Education?

Directions for Scoring.

An answer of "No" has a value of 2; "Sometimes", or other qualified answers, a value of 1; and "Yes", a value of 0.

Rating Chart.

```
     100   - - Professional Paragon.
    95-99  - - Above normal.
    85-94  - - Normal.
    70-84  - - Sub-normal.
    60-74  - - Professionally chilled.
  Below 60 - - Completely frozen.
```

Fig. 2.2 Take your professional temperature quiz. (Nannie H. Burroughs, Papers of Nannie H. Burroughs, Library of Congress, *Take Your Professional Temperature*, undated, Box 311)

in an agenda from a staff meeting held November 8, 1941 where the following were recorded: reports, minutes, proposal, assignments, and remarks. In the meeting, Mrs. Etta Head, social science teacher, immediately voiced a concern about instruction, "The class seems to be unable to get into the text. All of my other classes are doing good work, and I am unable to diagnose the trouble with this class."[20] Mrs. Head appeared to be confounded by how to keep her class engaged in the topic. The meeting notes reflect that her colleagues suggested Mrs. Head try to motivate students using their own interests and to ensure variety in the presentation of her lecture topics. She agreed to allow her students to write their own questions and let other students answer peer-generated questions. Mrs. Gunn, a sewing teacher, brought a problem concerning student Miss Mildred Nixon to her colleagues' attention. Miss Nixon had apparently skipped a meeting with Mrs. Gunn about an assignment. Burroughs brought Miss Nixon into the meeting and admonished her about her responsibilities as a student and demanded that Miss Nixon not miss any future meetings with her teacher.[21] In Ms. Burroughs's interaction with her teachers, we see her negotiating the complexities of school leadership.

Ms. Burroughs's Vision of History Instruction at NTS

To examine how the alternative black curriculum developed, I analyzed the methods Nannie H. Burroughs and her teachers used to build a social studies program at NTS by looking at (1) how social studies was broadly defined at NTS, (2) how Nannie H. Burroughs integrated black history in the instructional program at NTS, and (3) how teachers responded to Burroughs's vision in their classroom instruction.

The National Training School for Women for Girls was advertised to outside donors as a school focused on providing girls with opportunities to work as domestic servants and secretaries. Walking the tightrope that many African American instructional leaders faced, the promotion of an "industrial education" was balanced with a surprisingly classical education for the students. The NTS social studies program offered a wide range of courses including US history, modern European history, ancient history, psychology, sociology, Negro history, and problems of American democracy.[22]

[20] Burroughs, *N.T.&P Teachers' Conference*, November 8, 1941, Box 311.
[21] Burroughs, *N.T.&P Teachers' Conference*, November 8, 1941, Box 311.
[22] Burroughs, *Liberal Arts Division-Courses Given*, Box 314.

Burroughs's social studies recommendations appeared to follow a sequence that was recommended by the Committee of Ten (1893) and the Committee of Seven (1916). Her textbook choices included *The History of Europe—Our Own Times*, by James Harvey and Charles Austin Beard; *Modern European Civilization*, by Hilton Walker; *American People*, by David Saville Muzzey, and *Leading Facts in American History*, by D.H. Montgomery. She also required *The Negro in Our History* and *The Story of the American Negro*, both written by Carter G. Woodson.[23]

Many of these works were heavily concentrated on the accomplishments of European civilizations. However, despite this traditional focus on the master narrative, Burroughs clearly envisioned a more expansive program for her girls. Beginning in the 1920s, she began to incorporate black history into the instructional program at NTS. Her collaboration with Carter G. Woodson and the International Council of Women of the Darker Races likely influenced Burroughs to begin establishing programs and resources that celebrated black history.

In constructing an alternative black curriculum in social studies, Nannie H. Burroughs combined the vision of teaching black history of Carter G. Woodson and W.E.B. Du Bois. She created a school committed to conveying a historical narrative with a particular focus on the arts. Throughout her tenure as an NTS instructional leader, Burroughs integrated historical narratives with visual and performing arts as a way to motivate students to learn. In an undated document entitled, "Our Music, We Sing at this School" the author wrote:

> The President [referring to Burroughs], of the training school realizes the value of our own music, and she takes time to teach students the value of our own songs and the art of singing them. She makes us feel the spirit of the songs, and develops in the entire school a real appreciation for what our race has done in the field of music.[24]

Throughout her career, Burroughs used the arts as a primary vehicle for transmitting the alternative black curriculum and to provide context for the black experience in the United States (Fig. 2.3).

In her initial experiment with incorporating black history, Burroughs targeted extracurricular activities like the annual Appreciation Days

[23] Burroughs, *Textbook Orders*, Box 311.
[24] Burroughs, *Our Music*, undated, Box 312.

OUR MUSIC

WE SING AT THIS SCHOOL

We love our music, This is not a mere statement. It is a fact. One of the most valuable and remarkable traits of ~~the Negro~~ our race is ~~his~~ our love for music. The world's greatest critics are fair. They say that the Negro's sense of rhythm and melody are most pronounced. The only original folk songs that America can boast of are the Negro Spirituals; and the only distinct and valuable contribution to Music that has been made by a race while it was in slavery, ~~is~~ is that which the Negro made when he was in bondage. These songs of ~~the Negro~~ our race express the deep emotions of ~~their~~ our souls without a note of hate.

The President of the Training School realizes the importance of music, and she takes time to teach students the value of our own songs and the art of singing them. She makes us feel the spirit of the songs, and develops in the entire school a real appreciation for what the race has done in the field of Music.

The students of this school have had and are still enjoying wonderful opportunities for appearing before some of the finest audiences and groups of distinguished people, including the now First Lady of the Land, Mrs. Herbert Hoover, Mrs Hoover ~~[illegible]~~ invited us to sing in her home, Young people from all races were present. The Training school ~~[illegible]~~ has a splendidly equipped music department.

Fig. 2.3 Our music—"We Sing at this School." (Nannie H. Burroughs, Papers of Nannie H. Burroughs, Library of Congress, *Our Music*, undated, Box 312)

where students spoke on the following topics: Lincoln's Gettysburg Address, Myrtilla Miner, African American Christian missionaries, Toussaint L 'Overture, and key achievements of African civilizations.[25] Of interesting note is that throughout Burroughs's work on the alternative black curriculum is a constant thread of how allies assisted African

[25] Myrtilla Miner was a white educator who founded the Normal School for Colored Girls in Washington DC.

Americans in their fight for freedom.²⁶ Each Appreciation Days program included references to Abraham Lincoln, John Brown, the Underground Railroad, and other key white abolitionists who served the cause of freedom. Although it appears that Burroughs attempted to create an atmosphere encouraging a love for black history outside the classroom, the content of the history classes remained relatively conservative. An examination of the final exams of secondary students revealed a primary concern with topics such as the accomplishments of Grecian democracy.²⁷ Even as Burroughs began to infuse her school with black history themes, her teachers were hesitant to fully abandon their attachments to a narrative reliant on the dominant culture.

Beginning in the 1930s, but most clearly present in the 1940s, a class in Negro history was developed. Burroughs's class in African American history was not unique. In the 1930s, many segregated black high schools began to adopt African American textbooks and Negro history courses.²⁸ By the late 1930s, African American students in segregated schools as far South as Mississippi could take elective courses in black history.²⁹ Burroughs's stand-alone class appeared in a master schedule of the school, along with a list of textbooks that had been purchased at NTS. In a photograph dated 1935, the words "This Room is for the Study of Negro History" are written proudly on the blackboard of one of her classrooms. Despite evidence of the course being taught in the building, it was difficult to determine the exact nature of what was being taught by instructors of that particular course (Fig. 2.4).³⁰

HISTORY TEACHERS AT NTS

Located within the Burroughs archives are the names of social studies instructors, the majority of which were women: Lena Jones, I. Orontes Woods, E.J. Bonds, and Etta Head all who served the school from the

---

²⁶ Burroughs, *Appreciation Day Programs*, Box 312.
²⁷ Burroughs, *History Tests*, 1920–1921, Box 311.
²⁸ Jonathan Zimmerman. *Whose America? Culture Wars in the Public Schools*. Cambridge: Harvard University Press.
²⁹ Ibid.
³⁰ Located within the digital collection of the Library of Congress, there is a classroom picture with a sign stating, "This room is for the study of Negro history." This photograph provided corroborating evidence that there was indeed Negro history being taught in this class: http://www.loc.gov/pictures/collection/coll/item/2004667312/.

```
                    HOW WE HAVE BEEN HELPED
                         BY THE STUDY
                              OF
                        NEGRO HISTORY

        All Schools teach some kind of history; but all schools do not
   teach Negro history. This school teaches History and Negro History
   and the students are tremendously inspired by learning the truth
   about their own race.
        We learn  know now that our race has  been a valuable part of all that has been
   going on in the building of world civilizations. Dr. Carter G.
   Woodson's books are used as the text here and we have a room, a real
   library – if you please – set apart for the Study of Negro Life and
   History. If you want to see us in our glory visit us on Appreciation
   Day, February 23nd, and hear us tell what the Negro has done for the
   world and what has been done by some people for the Negro.
        We want to enter a contest in Negro history with some other
   School because when it comes to this race history and hokum the
   Training School Girls have the world beat, not including Dr. Woodson,
           however,
    Come on, a students of other
    schools & we'll clean up
    with you. We know our
    material.
```

Fig. 2.4 How we have been helped by Negro history. (Nannie H. Burroughs, Papers of Nannie H. Burroughs, Library of Congress, Box 312)

1920s through the 1950s. Challenged by Burroughs to implement her vision, teachers left the central artifacts of their craft, lesson plans and final exams, for our review. Embedded within the lesson plans is an approach to a history narrative and pedagogy that was quite conservative. Moreover, a review of final assessments administered to students during the 1920–1921 academic year provides a glimpse of the type of knowledge the social studies teachers valued.

I. Orontes Woods's US history final exams covered the following topics: nullification, John. C. Calhoun, Henry Clay, Daniel Webster, tariffs, Missouri Compromise, Battle of New Orleans, and the incident on the ships the Monitor and the Merrimac. Obviously, these topics are not representative of the entire body of work Woods taught; however, they do provide some idea about the information Woods valued. As part of the final examination, Woods required students to answer fill in the blank questions:

> Who Said----
> "Our Federal Union! It must be preserved"!
> "I can scarcely contemplate a more incalculable evil than the breaking of the Union into two or more parts."

This form of assessment mirrored the traditional pedagogical approach in history.[31]

Pauline Oberdorfer's first preparatory class focused on the early events of US history. On her final exam, she asked about Sir Walter Raleigh and the settlement of Roanoke Island. She also taught about Native Americans and the colony of Jamestown. In this section, the only direct reference to the history of African Americans was a question on the arrival of slaves to Jamestown. She mentions the first slaves' arrival to the New World but does not offer a complete history of the early role that Africans played in Jamestown. In the early period of NTS, the curriculum maintained a very specific focus on traditional US history narratives.

Lena Jones taught ancient history courses in which wide-ranging information was introduced to her students. The existence of a junior normal class, which prepared students for teaching, was far more comprehensive in the breadth and depth of the curriculum, even in its traditional form, than a skilled domestic would need to perform her duties. In her junior normal class, she taught early civilizations, and she expected her students to probe deeply into early English history. She asked students to classify the rulers of England up to Edward I, key early literary pieces in England, Richard I, and the story of the Holy Grail. In the school year 1920–1921, her second normal class learned about Egypt, Babylonia, Assyria, Phoenicia,

---

[31] Burroughs, *History Tests*, 1921–1922, Box 311.

Palestine, and Greece. Her students learned key figures in ancient history including but not limited to Hippocrates, Erastosthenes, Euclid, Manetho, Draco, and Pericles (Figs. 2.5, 2.6 and 2.7).

Students at NTS were expected to memorize significant details about the past in line with what other academic high schools and normal schools were teaching during the period from 1890–1940.[32] During the 1920–1921 school year, teachers did not include African American history in the final exams nor is there any reference to a Negro history class until 1929. By the late 1920s, Burroughs appears to have become more confident in her own understanding of black history. One must wonder if Burroughs shared her increasing knowledge with her teaching staff or whether her increased involvement in the study of African American history in that era was a personal journey.

In assessing the lesson plans and tests at NTS two decades later, significant patterns and trends emerged including focused instruction on topics such as the differences between Southern, Middle, and New England colonies and key geographic features of early America.[33] In the 1940s, Etta J. Head taught US history, problems of American democracy, senior high world history, and psychology at NTS. The problems of American democracy course explored the history of labor unions. On a test administered May 8, 1942, a glimpse into World War II content related to the history and formation of labor unions is provided. Students were asked to define labor union, trace the development of the labor movement in America, discuss the impact of the New Deal on the labor movement, and trace the extent of unemployment from 1920 to 1933. The final exams reveal that students at NTS were engaged in active examination of current events and problems in history, as well as understanding the key events of the past. Throughout the WWII era in the United States, similar courses to Ms. Head's *Problem of American Democracy* course were being taught, much to the consternation of their conservative critics.[34] Ms. E.J. Bonds was also a teacher of US history during this period. The multitasker of the staff, Ms. E.J. Bonds, also taught Secretarial Subjects and Math. In her history class, Bonds focused on Geography, reviewing with students the

---

[32] Burroughs, *History Tests, Junior Normal Class*, 1920–1921, Box 311.
[33] Burroughs, *Etta Head Lesson Plans*, December 1,3,5 1941, Box 311; Burroughs, E.J. Bonds *Lesson Plans*, undated, Box 311.
[34] Zimmerman, *Whose America? Culture Wars in the Public Schools*, 64–65.

ANCIENT HISTORY

First Normal Class

1. Of what does Ancient History treat?
2. Name the divisions of the Prehistoric Times; the divisions of the Historic Times.
3. What is meant by castes?
   How is the caste in each of the following countries classified:- Great Britain, United States, and India?
4. In what countries are the following cities: Tyre, Jerusalem, Nineveh, Damascus, Alexandria, Sidon, Ur, Susa, Accod, and Memphis.
5. State a fact about each of the following: Menes, Menepiatha, Khufu, Assurbanifal, Abraham, Moses, Samuel, Croesus, Cyrus, and Belshazzar.
6. Classify: Medes, Persians, Germans, Greeks, Romans, Hebrews, Phoenecians, Assyrians, Chaldeans, Arabs, and Egyptians.
7. Who was the first king of the Kingdom of Israel?
   How long did the above kingdom exist?
   Contained how many tribes?
   Who led it into exile?
8. Tell who was the first king of the Kingdom of Judah?
   How long did it exist?
   Contained how many tribes?
   Who finally led it into exile?
9. Name in order the six steps in Oriental History.
10. What is the contribution of Egypt, Babylonia, Assyria, India, China, Phoenicia, Palestine, and Persia to civilization.

L. L. Jones

Fig. 2.5 Ancient history. (Nannie H. Burroughs, Papers of Nannie H. Burroughs, Library of Congress, *History Tests*, 1920–1921, Box 311)

[Handwritten lesson plan reproduced from the Collections of the Manuscript Division, Library of Congress]

> Subject: U. S. History – Elson
> Classes: First and Second High School
> Subject Matter: Chapter VII
> Nature of Study:
>   Mon: Oral recitation
>   Wed: Test Chapter VII Papers Virginia vs New England
>   Fri: Unit VII Science Oral recitation
>
> Subject: Jr. College History
> Classes: Jr. College
> Subject Matter: Chapters VI and VII
> Nature of Study:
>   Mon: Oral recitation
>   Wed: "   "
>   Fri: Write a paper in class. The Growth of the Population in Cities. Cause Problem Solution Result
>
> Subject: World History
> Classes: Third and Fourth High School
> Subject Matter: Chapter III IV
> Nature of Study:
>   Mon: Test
>   Wed: Begin Ch. IV Oral recitation
>   Fri: Continue Ch. IV

Fig. 2.6 US history exams. (Nannie H. Burroughs, Papers of Nannie H. Burroughs, Library of Congress, *History Tests*, 1920–1921, Box 311)

importance of cotton and linen to the American economy and the invention of the cotton gin.

Although there were challenges linking lesson plans to a specific teacher, the unidentified lesson plans still offer insight into the world of NTS. One such plan of an unnamed teacher focused on the foundations of early

ENGLISH, HISTORY, GEOGRAPHY and ARITHMETIC CLASSES
Week of December 1, 1941

ARITH. BOOK V.
(Mon.) 5th Grade (Marian and Doris) Bring in pp. 26-27.
Review pp. 17-25....per need.

6th Grade (Dolores, Rebecca and Addie) BOOK VI. (pp. 32-37)

7th " (Thelma, Dorothy, Carmeta) BOOK VI.
Bring in pp. 50-51
Class assignment - pp. 56-57

TU. Continue unfinished problems...and review.
Wed. MATHEMATICAL CONTEST on ANALYSIS.
Thu. Written Test.
Fri. Correlation of week's assignments with previous work.

U.S.HISTORY: M^on. Dramatization of Chapters 7-10, ad lib.
Tu. (Tu.) Read and Discuss Chapter 11.
Wed. Questions on Chapter 11.
Thu. Letters on Chapter 11 (Journalizing)
Fri. True-False Test on Chapters 10-11.

GEOGRAPHY: Review of Cotton and Linen. The Cotton Gin, (Charter)
Cotton seed. Flax.

Wool and its origin. Countries produced in.
Qualities and by-products.

ENGLISH:
Monday, Talk about Test Papers.
Tu. Review. SPELLING:
Wed........ pp. 29-31, Follow instructions.
Thu. Review individual needs. Difficult wordsi
Fri. pp. 32-33 Oral and Written. in all subjects.

STANDARD HOME WORK: HISTORY QUESTIONS (in back of book) for each
day's work.... per assignment.

ARITHMETIC -- Bring in problems from each
day's lesson.

SPELLING:--Write all misspelled words 10 times.

Fig. 2.7 English, history, geography, and arithmetic classes. (Burroughs, Nannie H. Papers of Nannie H. Burroughs, Library of Congress, *History Tests*, 1920–1921, Box 311)

American history. The topics addressed included Cortes's invasion of Mexico, the awakening of early exploration in Europe, and early American institutions such as the House of Burgesses, the Mayflower Compact, and Declaration of Independence. Clearly, the master narrative was being conveyed to students. Twenty years after the 1920–1921 final exams were administered, there were still parts of social studies instruction that remained quite connected to a traditional approach to understanding history.[35]

Ancient history courses seemed to focus on learning about early Asian history, the Old Stone Age, Egypt, Babylonia, Persia, and Jewish history. Frequent use of textbooks was encouraged with students being told to examine books and answer questions. The tension between Burroughs's expansive vision of history and the everyday challenge of teaching and learning is present. The staff at NTS appeared to be seeking a balance of nurturing a love for black history with the reality that students would need to understand key themes about the master narrative.

In 1946, Mrs. Carter taught a stand-alone course in Negro history.[36] This is not the first time such a course appears in the school records. Prior to appearing on the schedule, the course was mentioned in the 1929 student annual. Its presence on the student schedule in 1946 is evidence that the Negro history course became part of the social studies curriculum being provided at the school. Unfortunately, since there are no remaining lesson plans or tests, it is difficult to discern the exact nature of the narrative being taught in the course. What is clear, however, is that Negro history was not infused in the regular history curriculum at NTS. It stands to reason that the narrative of the American and Ancient history courses remained quite conservative at NTS because teachers may have believed that the Negro history course immersed students in new narratives of black history.

The pedagogical methods at NTS were typical of teachers during the early twentieth century with oral recitation being utilized as the primary pedagogy.[37] David Tyack described the prevalent use of recitation in schools at the turn of the century (Figs. 2.8, 2.9 and 2.10):

---

[35] Burroughs, *E.J. Bonds Lesson Plans*, undated, Box 311.
[36] Burroughs, *Teachers Reports*, Fall of 1949-Spring 1950, Box 311.
[37] John L. Rury, *Education and Social Change: Themes in the History of American Schooling* (Mahwah NJ: Lawrence Erlbaum Associates, 2002), 142–147.

Fig. 2.8 Double V. (Nannie H. Burroughs, Papers of Nannie H. Burroughs, Library of Congress, *The Negro Project by Miss Gloria Dunlap*, Box 166)

Through an elaborate system of graduation, programmed curriculum, examinations, and rules for "deportment," then, the pupil learned the meaning of obedience, regularity, and precision. He learned to "toe the line"-a phrase that today has lost its literal significance to most people. Joseph Rice, who visited hundreds of urban classrooms in the 1890s,

Fig. 2.9 Breaking down racial prejudice (The Negro Project). (Nannie H. Burroughs, Papers of Nannie H. Burroughs, Library of Congress, *Breaking down Racial Prejudice*, Box 166)

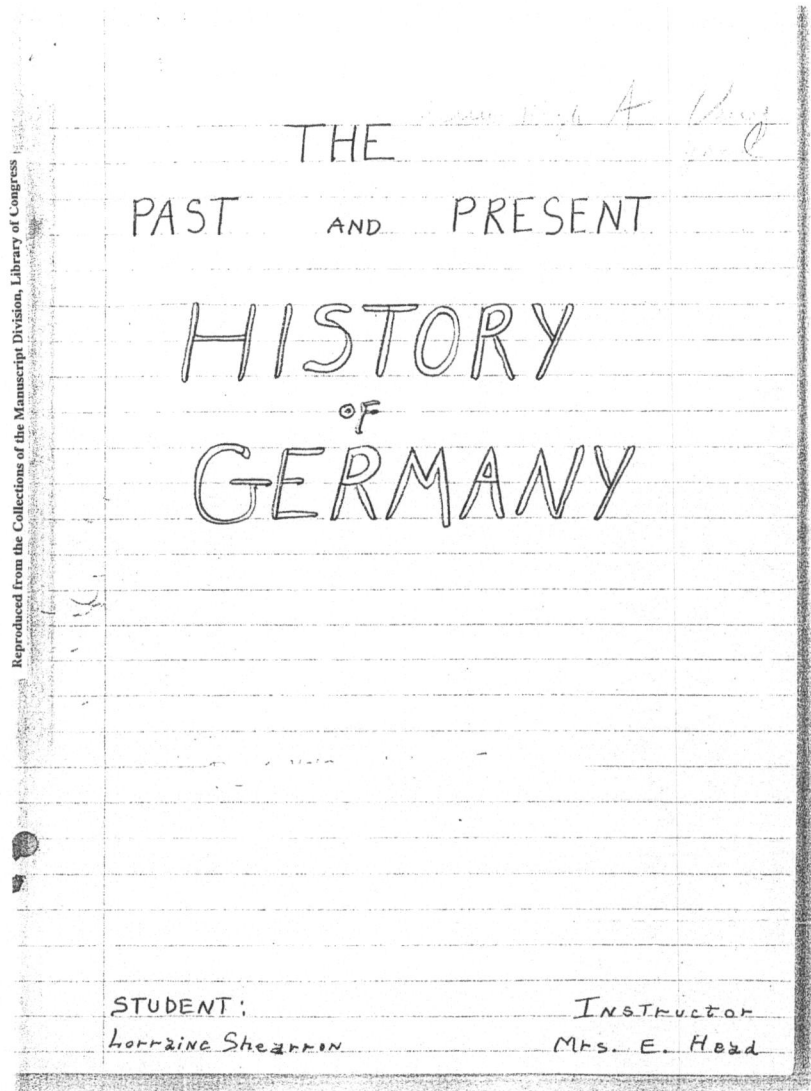

Fig. 2.10 The past and present history of Germany. (Nannie H. Burroughs, Papers of Nannie H. Burroughs, Library of Congress, *The Past and Present History of Germany by Miss Lorraine Shearron*, Box 166)

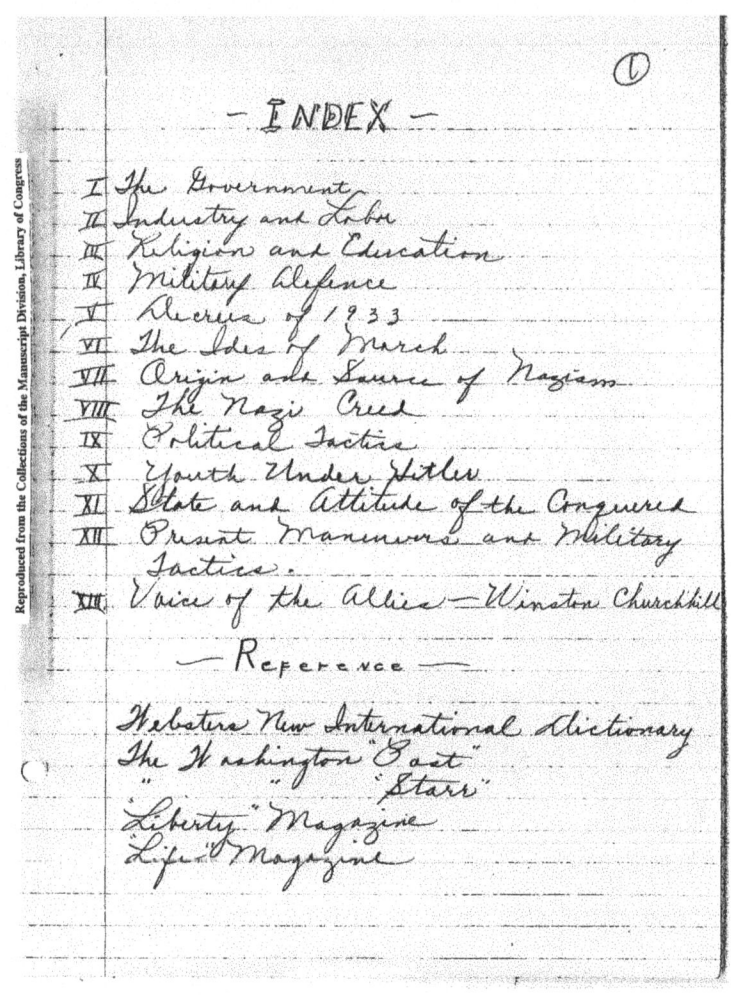

Fig. 2.10 (continued)

described what it meant in one school. During recitation periods, when students were to demonstrate that they had memorized the text, children were expected, said Rice, "to stand on the line, perfectly motionless, their bodies erect, their knees and feet together, the tips of their shoes touching the edge of the board in the floor."[38]

David Tyack's description of recitation is reflected as the primary pedagogy in most of the NTS lesson plans. The strict and conservative nature of the school likely led to the extensive use of this technique. However, in other parts of the lesson plans are glimmers of more participatory forms of learning. For example, in Ms. Bond's notes, there was mention of a simulation called a "Pioneer Party." In addition, one of Etta Head's students constructed an in-depth project on the heroic African American Navy Sailor, Dorie Miller.[39] So, despite the teachers' conservative leanings, there was some innovative pedagogy present to support student learning. In addition, there were multiple opportunities for the girls to participate in Appreciation Days, pageants, and clubs which reinforced the curriculum of the school in a much more compelling fashion.

---

[38] Burroughs, *E.J. Bonds Lesson Plans*, undated, Box 311.
[39] Burroughs, *Negro Project*, undated, Box 166.

CHAPTER 3

Black Curriculum in Social Studies: A Textual Reading of *When Truth Gets a Hearing*

In 1909, Nannie Helen Burroughs created the National Training School for Women and Girls in Washington, DC, which was designed to teach African American girls skills to be intellectual contributors to the nation's labor force. Historians of the National Training School have emphasized its conservatism, discipline, and adherence to the industrial Christian model.[1]

In this chapter, I focus on a little-known aspect of Nannie Helen Burroughs's role in the development of the alternative black curriculum: her creation of the historical pageant, *When Truth Gets a Hearing*. Through this analysis, I hope to ascertain how a woman author created a narrative which developed and nurtured the identities of African American girls. It is critical for scholars to explore how Nannie Helen Burroughs analyzed perspectives on womanhood and femininity. Burroughs's perspectives on the role of black women in history added wider scope to the alternative black curriculum. Finally, I demonstrate how Burroughs's pageant influenced subsequent pageants written by other less prominent black women educators.

According to extant records found in the Library of Congress, *When Truth Gets a Hearing*, acted by the students, was performed four times between 1916 and 1930. The Black-centered pageant challenges current historiography in four crucial aspects. First, a reading of *When Truth Gets*

[1] Ibid.

© The Author(s) 2018
A. D. Murray, *The Development of the Alternative Black Curriculum, 1890–1940*,
https://doi.org/10.1007/978-3-319-91418-3_3

a Hearing subverts traditional underpinnings of the nature of Nannie Helen Burroughs's philosophies of "training" Black girls for their "proper place" in the early twentieth-century White supremacist society.[2] Second, a reading of *When Truth Gets a Hearing* challenges current narratives about how the field of social studies was constructed and reconstructed to incorporate Black history.[3] Third, Nannie Helen Burroughs's work also challenges traditional epistemological frameworks of the field of social studies/history education. These interpretations have tended to emphasize the standards of social studies organizations such as the National Council of Social Studies. In contrast, Nannie Helen Burroughs, through her correspondence with Carter G. Woodson and the authoring of *When Truth Gets a Hearing*, reveals a case of how African American scholars actively sought to reshape social studies through the creation of an "unofficial" curriculum. Finally, Burroughs's work serves as a model of the types of pageants being produced by black women throughout the period 1890–1940. Her writing along with many others demonstrated how black women reshaped the Progressive Era pageant to meet the social and emotional needs of black children. In this alternative curriculum, history became a vehicle for uplifting, educating, and inspiring African American girls in the early part of the twentieth century (Fig. 3.1).

Often, scholarly literature about Burroughs portrays her as a female version of Booker T. Washington, exhorting African American women to a life of labor. In creating a vision for the National Training School for Women and Girls, which focused on training girls for positions of laundresses and secretaries, Burroughs seemed to remain loyal to Washington's vision. However, in *When Truth Gets a Hearing*, she imparted a more complicated message which included a passionate defense of Black intellectualism. Burroughs seemed quite aware that Black school leaders needed to communicate a varied message to their diverse audiences who ranged from White philanthropists to the parents of girls who attended her school.

Nannie Helen Burroughs's pageant *When Truth Gets a Hearing* demonstrates how African American educators reinterpreted available historical sources to create an alternative black curriculum challenging the dominant narrative institutionalized in all schools during the early twentieth century.

---

[2] Higginbotham, *Righteous Discontent*, 213.

[3] Carter G. Woodson, *The Mis-Education of the Negro* (Trenton: African World Press, 1990).

Fig. 3.1 *When Truth Gets a Hearing* (addition). (Nannie H. Burroughs, Papers of Nannie H. Burroughs, Library of Congress, *The Past and Present History of Germany by Miss Lorraine Shearron*, Box 166)

Throughout the course of this chapter, I will consider the context of the social studies curriculum, the impact of pageants in the black community and schools, a review of the literature on Nannie Helen Burroughs, and a textual analysis of the pageant *When Truth Gets a Hearing*.

THE SOCIAL STUDIES CANON AND AFRICAN AMERICAN RESPONSES

The field of social studies developed in the latter half of the nineteenth century. Debates over formal curriculum often reflected differing ideological conceptions regarding the proper role of social studies in a democracy. In 1893, the National Education Association (NEA) created a standardized curriculum to be taught in the nation's high schools. The Committee of Ten, chaired by Charles Eliot of Harvard University and led by a subcommittee composed of leaders such as Charles Kendall Adams, Woodrow Wilson, and James Harvey, drafted a social studies curriculum which profoundly shaped the social studies field.[4] In their final recommendations, they suggested a course of study that included a heavy focus on American history, Greek and Roman history, French history, and English history. In 1896, the American Historical Association (AHA) commissioned a group of historians to survey history instruction in the nation's public schools. Embracing social science methods, these historians conducted a comprehensive analysis of how history was being taught in school.[5] In 1916, another group of prominent educators, influenced by the educational philosophy of John Dewey, sought to refine the ideas suggested by the initial Committee of Ten. The group proposed a curriculum that stressed an ideological commitment to civics and democracy.[6] In each of the committees' recommendations, the history sequences placed a heavy value on the accomplishments of Europe.

Although progressive in their embrace of how history should be broadened to include more social history, the reformers tended to limit the types of narratives they embraced. The curricula stressed the narrative of Europe's, and by extension, the United States', domination over the supposedly "inferior" races of Africa, Asia, and Latin America. Moreover, each curriculum stressed a traditional narrative of the United States, emphasizing the founding of our country by a group of intelligent White men. This approach reified the racism that was prevalent in American society.[7]

Although African American historians were interested in larger Progressive Era education reform, they were more passionate about fighting the rampant Jim Crow endemic in American life. In an attempt to create an intellectual self-defense of black humanity, African American historians and educators

[4] David Jenness, *Making Sense of Social Studies*. (New York: Macmillan Publishing Company, 1990), 67. Ronald W. Evans, *The Social Studies War: What Should We Teach the Children?* (New York: Teachers College Press, 2004). Herbert M. Kliebard, *The Struggle for the American Curriculum* (New York: Routledge Falmer, 2004).
Thomas Fallace, "Did the Social Studies Really Replace History in American Schools?" *Teachers College Record* 110 (October 2008): 2246.
[5] Chara Bohan, "Early Vanguards of Progressive Education: The Committee of Ten, The Committee of Seven and Social Education," *Journal of Curriculum and Instruction* 19 (Fall 2003): 73-94.
[6] Jenness, *Making Sense of Social Studies*, 73.
[7] Terrie Epstein, *Interpreting National History: Race, Identity, and Pedagogy in Classrooms and Communities.* (New York: Routledge, 2008).

created an alternative black curriculum. The alternative black curriculum offered a critique of the normative structure of the dominant historical narrative. Organizations such as the Association for the Study of Negro Life, founded in 1915, and the National Association of Colored Women, founded in 1896, formed to discuss how to generate more accurate portrayals of African American history. W.E.B. Du Bois, Carter G. Woodson, Anna Julia Cooper, and Nannie Helen Burroughs were among many prominent intellectuals who generated new epistemologies about African Americans' contributions to history.

Recent historiographical inquiries into the development of a new historical narrative explore its emergence in the period 1900–1940. These inquiries tend to focus on the work of black male scholars. By concentrating on the professional black male historian with degrees from prestigious institutions such as Harvard University, the work of black women professionals is obscured. One goal of this work is to explore the development of the alternative black curriculum with a "bottom-up" historical framework examining how women without traditional access to knowledge production consumed and generated new understandings of social studies.[8] The site of school provided black women teachers, librarians, and administrators with significant latitude about how their students should be taught history.

Progressive Era Pageants and Black Women

The Progressive Era was extremely influential in the development of the alternative black curriculum, and pageants were a Progressive Era enterprise. In the shift from the public oratory of the nineteenth century, pageants served as an important link from an agrarian society to a more urbanized country.[9] White intellectual elites viewed pageants as critical to increasing patriotism and love for the arts. Black elites such as W.E.B. Du Bois, Anna Julia Cooper, and Mary Church Terrell echoed this view and

---

[8] Charles Payne, *I've Got the Light of Freedom: The Organizing Tradition and the Mississippi Freedom Struggle* (London: University of California Press, 1995), 2. A "bottom-up" approach focuses on the role of ordinary individuals and their role in history. In addition, a "bottom-up" approach focused on the contributions of women to the Civil Rights Movement.

[9] David Glassberg, *American Historical Pageantry: The Uses of Tradition in the Early Twentieth Century* (Chapel Hill: The University of North Carolina, 1990).

worked to spread this idea to the masses, viewing pageants as essential components in the development of an arts movement focused on uplifting black culture.

While often associated with the black arts, pageants also contained educative value. In alignment with the views of Progressive educators such as John Dewey and J. Stanley Hall, black educators believed that black children could express their curiosity and imagination in a pageant format.[10] Carter G. Woodson strongly believed that pageants could fit squarely into the center of civic life of schools and communities, publishing *Plays and Pageants for the Life of the Negro* in the 1930s. Woodson also believed that students on the elementary, middle, and high school levels could benefit from a re-telling of black history.[11] In the elaborate pageants performed in towns and cities, people of color were largely absent in many celebrations. Along with women and working-class whites, black people's roles were distorted or minimized. Women were portrayed only in the domestic sphere, and working-class folks were entirely absent. In many ways, the female architects of the alternative black curriculum sought to fight the sexist, classist, and racist tropes engrained in the pageant craze.

Black women as authors of pageants have been completely understudied. Pageants appealed to black women educators for a variety of reasons and were used to express central elements of the alternative black curriculum. Pageants provided black women with the opportunity to create within the structured confines of a sexist society. Nannie H. Burroughs's pageant is one of the earliest, but both Mary Church Terrell (*Phillis Wheatley, African Poetess*) and Anna J. Cooper (*From Servitude to Service*) wrote pageants during this period.

Primarily, pageants were used to provide a story of racial uplift for students. The communal setting of pageantry was extremely important to black women educators, and as such, pageants were natural vehicles to link school and community. They offered roles for students, communicated key historical messages, and involved diverse members of the community. There were pageants that included character personification and pageants that featured actual historical figures. In the development of the alternative black curriculum, both avenues were used to construct pageants.

---

[10] Glassberg, *American Historical Pageantry*, 57.

[11] Willis Richardson, ed., *Plays and Pageants from the life of the Negro* (Jackson: University Press of Mississippi, 1993).

Creating a Revisionist Curriculum

When Truth Gets a Hearing represents the type of pageants that social studies educators and other scholars created in the period between Reconstruction and World War I. It is situated in a historical era where pageants were in vogue as a form of cultural transmission. Embracing the popularity of pageants as a form of race pride, W.E.B. Du Bois penned *Star of Ethiopia* which opened in 1913 and celebrated the 50th anniversary of the Emancipation Proclamation. Du Bois believed that historical pageants served to connect the disciplines of art and history, particularly histories of the people of the African diaspora. *Star of Ethiopia* connected elements of African history, the Middle Passage, slavery, and Reconstruction into one sweeping narrative.[12] Burroughs served as one of the prominent educators on the organizing committee for *Star of Ethiopia* which could explain how she became inspired to write her own pageant.

When Truth Gets a Hearing represents an attempt by one Black female educator to use a pageant to uplift and educate African American girls. Burroughs's pageant combined an appreciation of the historical triumphs of Africans with contemporary problems African Americans were confronting in the United States. She embedded religious themes, racial disputes, rich musical traditions, an analysis of labor issues, a critique of lynching, and narratives of ancient and US history in the transcript. Moreover, When Truth Gets a Hearing challenged the assumed superiority of White culture. In the pageant, a group of African Americans are presented defending their humanity in a court of law. The witnesses are introduced as Injustice, Prejudice, Ignorance, and Error. On the prosecution side: Truth, Law, Peace, Goodwill, Fairplay, Justice, History, and Representatives of the Negro Race and Africa. The pageant structure allowed African Americans to create a response to the injustices that were prevalent during the period shortly before World War I. Burroughs also selected a pageant as a vehicle to express these images, which demonstrated her intent to engage audiences of students, possible donors, and laypeople.

In the 1916 *Report on the Committee on Social Studies of the Commission on the Reorganization of Secondary Schools*, members proposed a curriculum sequence that included a course entitled *European History to about the 1700's, Including the Discovery and Settling of America* in which students

---

[12] David Krasner, *A Beautiful Pageant: African American Theatre, Drama and Performance in the Harlem Renaissance, 1910–1927* (New York: Palgrave, 2002). 89.

were encouraged to learn about the accomplishments of ancient Greeks, the Roman Empire, the Exploration Age, and the rise of England and France as nation-states.[13] This type of course reflected the importance of European history in secondary school curricula in the early part of the twentieth century. In contrast, *When Truth Gets a Hearing*'s section on ancient history challenged traditional notions of how students were taught about the world predating 1500 BC. The pageant begins with Justice declaring, "History, give us the facts about the Negro's contribution to ancient civilization and to the development of the New World."[14] Burroughs provides the reader with a guide to implicit critiques of the traditional narrative by framing the opening of this section of the pageant with an emphasis on revisionist history.

In the early part of the pageant, Nannie Helen Burroughs constructs a narrative that parallels accomplishments in Greece and Rome with those in Egypt, Nubia, and Abyssinia (Ethiopia). Burroughs's perspective that Egyptians should be included in the black racial group in Africa was quite different from scholars who categorized Egyptians as Middle Eastern and Caucasian. She described how Africans created the Sphinx at Giza and the civilization of Meroe and Abyssinia. By emphasizing the role of race, Burroughs offered an immediate example of how African American scholars were trying to create a link to a past predating modern Europeans.[15] A critical tenet of alternative black curriculum was the acknowledgment of stories of Black leadership in the ancient world. This tenet is also actualized in Burroughs's comparison of African civilizations to the mythic European past.

Germany's history is referenced in the ancient history section of *When Truth Gets a Hearing* in comparison to African history where Burroughs wrote:

> In fact, [when] the Anglos were barbarians in northern Germany eating their food out of the skulls of their ancestors and using the bones of their dead for knives and forks, black men were at work building civilization in Africa.[16]

---

[13] Jenness, *Making Sense of Social Studies*, 73.
[14] Nannie H. Burroughs, *When Truth Gets a Hearing*, Papers of Nannie Helen Burroughs, Library of Congress.
[15] Burroughs, *When Truth Gets a Hearing*, 9.
[16] Burroughs, *When Truth Gets a Hearing*, 9.

This direct attack on European superiority represented an attempt to strengthen Burroughs's claims that African Americans were equal counterparts to Whites. During this period, while White historians sought to present history in an "objective" fashion, Black scholars and practitioners laid out facts in defense of African Americans' humanity and freedom.[17]

Burroughs also attempted to convey the rich tradition of scholarship on the African continent through her work—another aspect of the alternative black curriculum. Nineteenth-century scholars claimed Blacks lacked civilization; Burroughs connected African Americans to a past that included significant scholarly accomplishments. In *When Truth Gets a Hearing*, History declares:

> Justice, the best scholars and historians concede, after years of research and investigation, that Ethiopia, or Black men, gave learning to Egypt-Egypt to Greece-Greece to Rome-Rome to Britain-and Britain to the world. This face, therefore gives the Negro a high place in the intellectual and political history of the world.[18]

Burroughs attacked the idea that African Americans were intellectually inferior to their White counterparts by arguing that Ethiopia and Egypt gave learning to the Greeks.

When Truth Gets a Hearing was written in subsequent drafts between 1916 and 1921, and clearly the events of the interwar period impacted Burroughs' analysis. In the US history portion of the pageant, similar themes to the section on ancient history emerged in Burroughs's writing. Evident in the US History section of the play is the focus on African American men's participation in the US military. Burroughs traced how Black men served in the Revolutionary War, the Civil War, Spanish-American War, and World War I, and she referenced the death of Crispus Attucks. Burroughs reinforced the message that African Americans had been loyal patriots. She wrote in the shadow of the Red Summer of 1919, when race riots occurred in the summer and fall.[19] The focus on Black males as citizens and patriots challenged notions of Black men as threats to White people of the United States.

---

[17] Peter Novick, *That Noble Dream: The "Objectivity Question" and the American Historical Profession* (Chicago: Cambridge University, 1987), 14.

[18] Burroughs, *When Truth Gets a Hearing*, 14.

[19] Howard Zinn, *The People's History of the United States: 1492–Present* (New York: Harper Perennial, 2003).

Nannie Burroughs also examined the contemporary issue of lynching. During the summer of 1919, blacks experienced a wave of violence which included clashes among the races, massacres, and lynching.[20] Addressing the controversial topic of lynching, Burroughs again demonstrated the subversive tendencies of the alternative black curriculum. In the section on lynching, Burroughs actively worked to connect racial violence with a lack of enforcement of the Thirteenth, Fourteenth, and Fifteenth Amendments. Burroughs, through the character, Legislation, explained:

> Justice, I am Legislation. I am here to speak for the enforcement of all laws.
> This government has spent millions of dollars for the enforcement of the eighteenth Amendment and not <u>one cent</u> for the enforcement of the 14th and 15th Amendments. It is more important that men have the <u>liberty</u> in America, than it is for them to not have liquor."[21]

Immediately after discussing issues of legislation, Burroughs referenced the lynching report created by the Commission on Interracial Cooperation. The Commission on Interracial Cooperation was established to investigate race riots that occurred in the summer of 1919.[22] By referencing these events in the pageant, Burroughs created a forum for her audience to contemplate meanings of African American citizenship in the face of racist conditions.

Burroughs also focused on the labor of slaves which she claimed was a crucial component in the establishment of the United States. Burroughs's character, Negro Womanhood, stated, "I felled trees, tilled fields, protected homes, nursed the children of another race, made brick, built big houses for others and cabins for myself."[23] In her section on labor, Burroughs sought to combat the stereotype that African Americans lacked a work ethic. A central premise of the National Training School for Women and Girls was its emphasis on the role women's hard work played in uplifting the black community. Nannie Helen Burroughs championed the idea of work throughout her life. Secondly, in *When Truth Gets a Hearing*, she encouraged African Americans to be proud of their work ethic. In fact, her

---

[20] Leon Litwack, *Trouble in Mind: Black Southerners in the Age of Jim Crow* (New York: Vintage Books: 1998), 7.
[21] Burroughs, *When Truth Gets a Hearing*, 35a.
[22] Robert L. Blaustein and Robert L. Zangrando. eds., *Civil Rights and the American Negro: A Documentary History.* (New York: Washington Square Press: 1968).
[23] Burroughs, *When Truth Gets a Hearing*, 17.

reliance on references to Christianity shows that Burroughs clearly wanted to connect the Protestant doctrine to the work that Blacks consistently were required to do throughout the history of the republic.

Negro Womanhood Defined

In the development of a black historical narrative, Nannie H. Burroughs's work shared similarities with narratives posited by black male historians such as W.E.B. Du Bois and Carter G. Woodson. Pero Gaglo Dagbovie discussed how black women served as practical implementers of the alternative black curriculum.[24] Burroughs and many other black women educators not only implemented the alternative black curriculum in their school but also added to key discourses about the history of African Americans in the United States. Much like her male colleagues, Nannie H. Burroughs appeared interested in uplifting and defending the black race through history. However, Burroughs added to the narrative by conceptualizing the role of black womanhood in US and world history quite differently through her pageant.

One of the explicit themes both Du Bois and Burroughs considered in their pageants was the impact that black women had on US and ancient history. In the *Star of Ethiopia*, Du Bois idealized the image of a saintly African American woman. He created a character, the Veiled Woman, who appeared throughout the pageant, symbolizing the dignity and splendor of black womanhood:

> At last dimly enhaloed in mysterious light, the Veiled Woman appears, commanding in stature and splendid in garment, her dark face faintly visible, and in her right hand fire, and iron her left.[25]

Du Bois attempted to provide black women an exalted status. However, throughout *Star of Ethiopia*, he continued to provide his male characters such as Mansa Musa, Stephen Dorantes, Toussaint L'Ouverture, John Brown, and Frederick Douglass far more agency in the fight against oppression and racism. In Du Bois's framing of black

---

[24] Pero Gaglo Dagbovie, "Black Women, Carter G. Woodson, and The Association for the Study of Negro Life and History, 1915–1950," *The Journal of African American History* 88 (2003): 30.

[25] *The Star of Ethiopia*, by W.E.B. DuBois, directed by Charles Burroughs, New York, October 1913.

history, black womanhood became idealized. As a result, black women lost their potency as equal advocates to men in promoting freedom in the African American community.

Nannie H. Burroughs conceived the role of black women quite differently. She explicitly mentioned the impact of the Queen of Sheba and Candace, Queen of Meroe, leaders of kingdoms in ancient civilization. Although she praised the accomplishments of black women, she also mentioned specific moments in history that provided clearer shape to women's work. More explicitly, she gendered the role of black labor. The dynamic was illustrated in one particular passage:

> Truth: Justice, this is an ex-slave. Will you let (her) tell her about her contribution to the up building of America.[26]

In the pageant, the character, ex-slave, delivered a speech about black women's labor, placing the work of black women squarely on an equal status with black men. So, in Burroughs's vision of the alternative black curriculum, women's agency played a critical role. Instead of idealizing the black woman, she explicitly argued about the concrete contributions of African American to the construction of black nationhood.

One of the unique characteristics of *When Truth Gets a Hearing* is Nannie Helen Burroughs's deliberate inclusion of and reference to the role of Black women in history. African American women in the Post-Reconstruction Era struggled to define themselves in both the private and public sphere. Throughout her pageant, Burroughs seeks to create a narrative that views Black women as significant contributors to their community.[27]

The ancient history section of *When Truth Gets a Hearing* stresses the establishment of the role of Black women as creators in history. Burroughs writes about Candace, queen of the Meroe civilization. When the Meroe civilization was ruled by a line of "queens" they were also known as a *candace* or *kandake*.[28] With this, Burroughs attempted to establish that women of color have always served as leaders in their communities. Burroughs may have included this perspective that highlighted

---

[26] Burroughs, *When Truth Gets a Hearing*, 17.

[27] Stephanie Shaw, *What a Woman Ought to Be and to Do: Black Professional Women During the Jim Crow Era* (Chicago: The University of Chicago Press, 1996).

[28] G. Mokhtar, *General History of Africa: Ancient Civilizations of Africa* (Berkley: Unesco, 1990), 76.

the accomplishments of Black women because she, herself, served as a leader in a predominantly African American setting. Burroughs sought to create figures and images that supported and uplifted her students. Indeed, Burroughs subverted common ideologies of women relegated to the home. *When Truth Gets a Hearing* directly supported the idea that African American girls must serve their world outside of the domestic sphere. Burroughs publicly emphasized the connection between labor and the Black woman, since the National Training School was reliant on outside philanthropists. The use of Candace, however, points to a subtler message that Black women had royal traits and heritage and could be leaders beyond the narrowly circumscribed roles as domestics that were the focus of much industrial education.

In her section on US history, Burroughs also extended the alternative black curriculum, which was often concerned with a defense of African American contributions, to a defense of Black womanhood on the North American continent. Burroughs wrote:

> I represent Negro Womanhood. For 250 years I worked in the cornfields, kept the big house like a palace, nursed the children of my master and loved them with a love and tenderness such as the world has never seen and will never see again.[29]

Here, Burroughs acknowledges the role labor played in African American women's identity. Again, she offered a counter-narrative to the role that women and Black women were often relegated to in segregated America. She called for Black women's work to be recognized. Burroughs's perspective is complicated by her reliance on the common sentimentality of the slave woman and their care of White children, which was associated with images of Southern womanhood during that period.

COMPARING *WHEN TRUTH GETS A HEARING* TO OTHER PAGEANTS

Nannie H. Burroughs's *When Truth Gets a Hearing* is one of the earliest pageants written by black women. However, themes explored in *When Truth Gets a Hearing* resonated in other pageants being produced in the period 1890–1940. In the book, *Plays and Pageants from the Life of the*

---

[29] Burroughs, *When Truth Gets a Hearing*, 28.

Negro, edited by Carter G. Woodson, three pageants by black women are referenced: *Out of the Dark* by Dorothy C. Guinn, *Two Races* by Inez Burke, and *The Light of the Women* by Frances Gunner. Each of these pageants share similarities and differences with *When Truth Gets a Hearing* and exhibited characteristics of the alternative black curriculum in social studies.

Dorothy C. Guinn, an Executive Director in the YWCA, co-created *Out of the Dark* in 1924. Her pageant was meant to be performed by high school students. It was published by the Women's Press based in New York. Guinn connected with a historical African past, writing:

> Mine is the role to tell the tale of a people who, having lived for ages of the dim past in that vast unknown land of the Sphinx, Africa, were brought against their will to another clime. How little do we know of their past culture![30]

She also utilized character personifications, introducing the role of the "Chronicler" who led the audience through significant stages in black history. The first part of the pageant describes the capture of black people from Africa. The second portion illuminated slavery in the United States until after Reconstruction. She finalized her pageant with the contributions of modern-day African American leaders. Similar to Burroughs, her pageant taught a layered history to black children then the curriculum they were receiving at schools.[31]

Guinn immediately situates her pageant in an African past. Structurally, she used dramatic interludes and tableaux to organize the pageant. She mentioned better known figures such as Booker T. Washington to highlight the importance of blacks in the early colonial period. However, she also created speaking parts for more obscure figures such as Alfred Alexander Smith and William Stanley Braithwaite. Guinn's pageant aligns with Burroughs vision in that it creates a very specific story of African American history. Guinn's pageant serves to teach young people a history that most white people would not recognize or acknowledge. Dorothy Guinn closed her pageant with specific instructions outlining how it could be staged in a school setting. She intended for her pageant to be utilized with multiple audiences.

[30] Dorothy C. Guinn, "Out of the Dark," in *Plays and Pageants from the life of the Negro*, ed. Willis Richardson (Jackson: University of Mississippi, 1993), 305–333.
[31] Guinn, "Out of the Dark," 311.

Inez Burke's pageant, *Two Races*, is starkly different from Guinn's. However, her pageant connects with *When Truth Gets a Hearing* in that it covers the impact of race and racism on the re-telling of history in the United States. It is difficult to find information about Inez Burke beyond the notes in *Plays and Pageants*, but what is known is that Burke was an elementary school teacher in the Washington DC area. *Plays and Pageants* was to be performed in 12 minutes for children in the seventh and eighth grades. The pageant is organized around two young children, Gilbert and Sam. Unlike *Out of the Dark*, this pageant took place in modern-day Washington DC.[32] The pageant starts out with a conversation between two young students:

Sam (black child): Don't you think my people out a little?
Gilbert (white child): Well, it isn't in these books. The only thing that I saw that your people have done is work as slaves on the plantations.[33]

This limited conversation is probably the most relatable to young students of all the pageants chronicled in this section. The goal of *Two Races* is to educate Gilbert about black peoples' accomplishments. The theme of having white allies is a critical element in this pageant, and this pageant is the first with explicit use of a white character. Burke uses the vehicles of Adventure, Invention, Slavery, Bravery, Oratory, Poetry, and Music to accomplish her goals. She emphasized the typical catalog of important black leaders: Benjamin Banneker, Crispus Attucks, and Frederick Douglass. However, she also emphasized lesser known individuals such as Jan Matzeliger, Granville T. Woods, Harry T. Burleigh, Will Marion Cook, and Flora Batson. By the end of the pageant, Gilbert transformed into an ally in the struggle with his increased knowledge of the black community. Much like Burroughs's *When Truth Gets a Hearing*, Burke makes a compelling case that white allies are important to black freedom.[34]

---

[32] Inez M. Burke, "Two Races," in *Plays and Pageants from the life of the Negro*, ed. Willis Richardson (Jackson: University of Mississippi, 1993), 295–305.
[33] Burke, "Two Races," 297.
[34] Burke, "Two Races," 295–305.

Finally, Frances Gunner's *The Light of the Women* continued Burroughs's rebuttal to male sexism about the centrality of black women's struggle to the reimagining of black history.[35] In this 20-minute pageant, Gunner uses Ethiopia to emphasize the journey of black women in the New World, writing:

> I bring good news, news light among the women. Light amid darkness; light amid care and sorrow; light amid prejudice and ignorance; light amid prejudice and ignorance; light amid oppression and cruelty; light down the shadows of the years; the light of the souls of good women; light from the Light of the World![36]

The pageant was created for use with junior high school girls and was also published by The Woman's Press. Gunner, also an executive in the YWCA, explicitly developed this pageant to develop black girls' pride, link the pageant movement to the clubwomen service, and respond to the racism of the white female suffrage movement.[37]

Black women educators clearly understood they were role models for young students, and the use of pageants emphasized methods for black girls to overcome racism in their lives and community. Frances Gunner created a black women's history mirroring Burroughs's which began on the continent of Africa and ended with the modern contributions of black women. She also grounded her narrative in a Christian tradition describing the work of evangelist Amanda Smith who traveled throughout America, England, Scotland, and India. Gunner ended the pageant with a discussion of the work of black women as teachers, doctors, ministers, and social workers. She also connected black women with the efforts in World War I. Gunner's vision values black women's service to the larger community. Both Gunner and Burroughs are explicit about the message that the heart of black girls was key to rebuilding the black community in the twentieth century.[38]

---

[35] Frances Gunner, "The Light of the Women," in *Plays and Pageants from the life of the Negro*, ed. Willis Richardson (Jackson: University of Mississippi, 1993), 336–345.

[36] Gunner, "The Light of the Women," 336.

[37] Christine R. Gray, "Introduction," in *Plays and Pageants from the life of the Negro*, ed. (Jackson: University of Mississippi, 1993), viii–xxxix.

[38] Gunner, "The Light of the Women," 333–345.

Conclusion

Black male citizenship in the period of 1815–1940 was defined by three common elements. The characteristics of black male citizenship included continual resistance toward colonization, a fight for suffrage, and access to basic accommodations. The pinnacle of the fight for black male citizenship battle is reached when black males participate actively during the Civil War. In these early struggles for citizenship, black women's participation was limited at best. However, with the conclusion of the Civil War and the rebuilding of the black community during the Reconstruction period, black women began to develop a definition of citizenship that was shaped by different parameters.

However, it is the access to consistent paid (albeit low) teaching positions, which allowed middle-class black women to expand notions of what it meant to be a citizen in the early twentieth century. Central to new definitions of citizenship was uplifting and education of black children. Through teaching, black women began to recognize that education played an essential role in creating active and involved participants in a democracy. Black women recognized in order to fully participate in a democracy, black children must be equipped with reading, writing, and computational skills to actively contribute to the black community. However, black women understood on a deeper level that the black citizenship also aligned with a comprehensive and a complete interpretation of black history. The pageant, with its intense focus on accurately portraying black history in its full complexity, represented a means for black women educators to create a compelling argument for access to rights under the Fourteenth Amendment.

Black women characterized the citizenship in different ways than black males. Their understandings of citizenship included participation and access in the public sphere via clubwomen activities, the demand for voting rights for women, and an accurate re-telling of American and world history. The pageants studied in this chapter represented a clarion call for women being actively involved in shaping a distinct twentieth century understanding citizenship.

CHAPTER 4

Resisting the Master Narrative: Building the Alternative Black *Counter-Canon*

Each year in classrooms across the nation, teachers shape for their students a narrative about the "history" of the United States. How is narrative conveyed in the classroom? Three key practices combine to create narratives in the classroom: the textbook, teacher training programs, and the curriculum.

Unfortunately, our "narrative" is often a simple one. This simple narrative, though, masks a larger debate over what knowledge should comprise the history of the United States. The epistemological battle over United States history engages a variety of players, including historians, education researchers, classroom teachers, parents, and politicians. These diverse political actors understand the stakes of this battle as the debate centers around several key questions: How do we define ourselves as a society? Whose individual voices matter? What should we value as American people? What are the roles of race and racism in the United States?

Quite often, we have told ourselves incomplete narratives that fail to fully account for the complex history of the United States. For instance, our narrative of the colonial period emphasizes the American Revolution as a triumph of Anglo-Saxon values in the modern age. This colonial narrative tells the story of the American Revolution guided by a select group of wise, knowledgeable "Founding Fathers"—Thomas Jefferson,

© The Author(s) 2018
A. D. Murray, *The Development of the Alternative Black Curriculum, 1890–1940*,
https://doi.org/10.1007/978-3-319-91418-3_4

George Washington, James Madison, and John Adams, who created a timeless Constitution.[1] This narrative, however, de-emphasizes the horrors of the Middle Passage. It fails to adequately acknowledge that the practice of slavery during the early colonial period was closely associated with the economy. Native Americans are depicted treated as rivals of English settlers, neglecting the story of the diverse cultural, political, and social lives of the many Native American cultures encountered during the colonial era.[2]

Historian Anthony Brown suggests that these simple narratives are incomplete, often rendering African Americans as absent from the history of the United States or having only minimally contributed to larger American society. The most infamous "simple" narrative is the history of Reconstruction, the period directly after the Civil War (1865–1877).[3] While the causes and effects of Reconstruction are heavily disputed, Progressive Era historians crafted a narrative that claimed the political inadequacy of the Radical Reconstruction could be traced to an attempt to build an interracial coalition between African American citizens and Northern White Republicans. The Dunning School of historians depicted the end of Reconstruction and the imposition of segregation as a success, with whites restored to predominate Southern hierarchy.[4] The incomplete narrative of Reconstruction has such a negative effect because it was placed in the key canonical text of the social studies curriculum: the in-class textbook. Just as the English teacher conveys the canon of American literature texts, the history teacher uses the textbook to convey a canon unique to their discipline. The textbook represents the most critical and common tool teachers use to transmit the dominant narrative.

Initially, most historians and education researchers agreed that the textbook is almost devoid of any "real history," or perhaps more accurately, "academic" history. For example, Bruce VanSledright argued that the "[r]hetorical hedges, interpretive discussion, evidence trials, and concerns"

---

[1] Jesus Garcia, Donna M. Ogle, and C. Frederick Risinger, eds., *Creating America: Beginnings through Reconstruction* (Geneva, CH: Houghton-Mifflin, 2008).

[2] Gary B. Nash, "The 'Convergence' Paradigm in Studying Early American History," in *Knowing, Teaching, and Learning: National and International Perspectives*, eds., Peter B. Sexias, Sam Wineburg, and Peter Stearns (New York: The New York University Press, 2000), 103–120.

[3] Wayne Au, Anthony Brown, and Dolores Calderon, *Reclaiming the Multicultural Roots of the U.S. Curriculum: Communities of Color and Official Knowledge in Education* (New York: Teachers College Press, 2016).

[4] Novick, *That Noble Dream*, 61.

about conflicting archival sources so common to historical scholarship are typically shorn from the books.[5] Consequently, the historical narrative around methodological and ideological approaches that characterized academic history is missing. Moreover, as Frances Fitzgerald notes in her classic study of textbooks, *America Revised*, textbooks reflect the institutional racism insofar as ethnic groups' struggles are simply invisible. Fitzgerald states:

> In the nineteen-thirties, the most progressive of social histories, the Rugg books, identified "the Negro" as a "social problem"; Rugg, as one might expect, counseled tolerance and an appreciation of the contributions made by such men as Booker T. Washington and Paul Robeson. The Rugg books were exceptional in this respect; few books published then or earlier noted the existence of blacks in contemporary America and still fewer recorded the name of an individual.[6]

Finally, the canonical textbooks often do not grasp a key rhetorical strategy of recent historical work—the consideration of counter-narratives. The emergence of a historical counter-narrative is an act that seeks to reclaim the treatment of a specific historical subject as an academic matter first, then later, a political act. For example, our changing understanding of the historical period of Reconstruction has been shaped by an emerging counter-narrative. The work of W.E.B. Du Bois in *Black Reconstruction* (1935), which developed a narrative that emphasized the role of black agency after the Civil War, as well as Charles and Mary Beard in *The Rise of American Civilization* (1930), which focused on the intricate class dynamics that characterized the Reconstruction period, were influential in creating a counter-narrative that challenged the dominant historical narrative of Reconstruction.[7] Creating an academic counter-narrative often has real and practical consequences such as in 1939 when the NAACP convened a committee that published a critique of school textbooks called *Anti-Negro Propaganda in School*.[8]

---

[5] Bruce VanSledright, "Narratives of Nation-State, Historical Knowledge, and School History Education," *Review of Educational Research* 32 (February 2008): 113.

[6] Frances Fitzgerald, *America Revised: History Schoolbooks in the Twentieth Century* (Boston: Little, Brown and Company, 1979), 83.

[7] James Loewen. *Lies My Teacher Told Me: Everything Your American History Textbook Got Wrong* (New York: Touchstone, 1995).

[8] Anthony Brown, "Counter-memory and Race," 55–63.

Given the importance of the creation process of the counter-narrative, the process of "narrative rewriting" of a counter-canon as a key part of the larger project of the alternative black curriculum must be considered. After considering the social studies canon of the Progressive Era, this chapter considers three interrelated concepts that led to the development of the alternative black curriculum. First, the chapter considers an emerging African American counter-canon as defined by the differing institutional visions of Carter G. Woodson and W.E.B. Du Bois. Second, this chapter independently considers the work of black women educators both in their shaping of the counter-canon and their work in also authoring key components of the counter-canon. Finally, this chapter explores *The Mis-Education of the Negro* and *Black Reconstruction* and their incorporation of foundational counter-canon concepts that are central to the alternative black curriculum.

THE AFRICAN AMERICAN COUNTER-CANON AND THE SOCIAL STUDIES CURRICULUM

A familiar idea in scholarly literature suggests that the field of social studies developed in the latter half of the nineteenth century. Debates over formal curriculum often reflected competing ideological conceptions over the proper role of social studies in a democracy. In 1893, the National Education Association (NEA) created a standardized curriculum for the nation's high schools. The Committee of Ten, chaired by Charles Eliot of Harvard University and led by a subcommittee composed of leaders such as Charles Kendall Adams, Woodrow Wilson, and James Harvey, drafted a curriculum that profoundly shaped the social studies field.[9] The final curriculum included a course of study with a heavy focus on American history, Greek and Roman history, French history, and English history.[10] In 1896, the American Historical Association (AHA) also commissioned historians to survey history instruction in the nation's public schools. Embracing social science methods, these historians, educators, and university presidents conducted a comprehensive analysis of the current state of historical studies in elementary and secondary schools. In 1916, another group of prominent educators, influenced by the educational philosophy of John Dewey, sought to refine the ideas suggested by the initial Committee of Ten. The group proposed a curriculum, which stressed an

---
[9] David Jenness, "Making Sense of Social Studies," 67.
[10] Chara Bohan, "Early Vanguards of Progressive Education," 73–94.

ideological commitment to civics and democracy. This group embraced social history as a methodological approach in the social studies curriculum, unlike the other approaches.[11]

The process of drafting these curriculums illustrated how mainstream social studies curriculum became a "canon" during the early twentieth century. First, these curriculums (supposedly) represented sophisticated historical methods treatment of social history. Despite how each committee varied in ideological predilections, all three proposed curriculums stressed the narrative of Europe's, and by extension as its sociocultural heir, the United States', domination over the "inferior" races of Africa, Asia, and Latin America. Moreover, all three curriculums stressed a traditional narrative history of the United States which emphasized the foundational events of the society as driven by the ambitions of white men. In this, the canon reflected and reified the systematic racism of the Progressive Era. Second, what we understood as "canon" emerged from the *institutionalization* of historical work during the Progressive Era. The institutionalization of historical work created new professional organizations that sought to refine the canon and, as the drafting of the curriculum demonstrates, to popularize newly refined work of the academy.

During the same period (1900 until 1940), African American historians and educators created a revisionist counter-canon. As with the "canon" itself, the counter-canon emerged in both intellectual and institutional forms. In its epistemological form, the counter-canon developed in many ways, culminating into two key texts, *The Mis-Education of the Negro* and *Black Reconstruction*. African American scholars, including Du Bois, Woodson, Cooper, and Burroughs, suggested new narratives for how world history and US history should be taught.

In its institutional form, the counter-canon developed through collaborative relationships between university and secondary school teachers. As previously discussed, this process appeared to be intensively gendered; primarily, male academics "inspired" female elementary and secondary school teachers. However, this process of enacting the African American counter-canon was a much more complex than that false binary between male academics and female secondary school figures. Instead, the process could be described as consensual insofar as both set of parties played a role in defining the intellectual content of the counter-canon as well as a role in building its institutional foundations.

[11] Jenness, "Making Sense of Social Studies," 73.

Building the Institutions of the African American Counter-Canon, 1900 until 1940

Carter G. Woodson and W.E.B. Dubois were the primary academic and organizational influences on building the African American counter-canon; however, each man envisioned the construction of the counter-canon in a different way. Woodson viewed creating the counter-canon as a process of building African American history as its own discipline. He emphasized building a framework to disseminate the discipline, including the development of textbooks and academic journals, the institution of Negro History (later to become Black History Month), and the development of the *Negro History Bulletin*, which would be widely disseminated to black elementary and secondary schools. By contrast, Du Bois's approach involved creating texts for the alternative black curriculum, focusing on the nexus between history, the arts, and literature. W.E.B. Du Bois was very interested in the educational supports that would nurture the development and self-esteem of black children. With this conception of the black child at the heart of his work, he viewed history as critical to nurturing a politically active child who would continue with their parents to struggle against racism.

This Section will first consider Woodson's collaborative efforts to build the *Negro History Bulletin*, and then turn toward Du Bois's work in building the African American canon through the publications of *The Crisis* and *The Brownies' Book*.

Carter G. Woodson and the Negro History Bulletin

Carter G. Woodson, a former secondary school teacher and the only immediate descendant of enslaved parents to receive a PhD, sought to "popularize" the study of black history. Woodson believed that the institutionalization of Black History through scholarly work and popularization was necessary to create the African American counter-canon. Notably, Woodson did not collaborate with women to develop his scholarly agenda. It appears that throughout the 1910s and the early 1920s, Woodson worked with a small group of primarily male colleagues, such as Lorenzo Greene, who produced articles that utilized a scientific approach to history. No evidence exists that Woodson mentored women scholars in a similar fashion; however, the process of "popular" institutionalization meant that Woodson constantly searched for collaborations with women educators who could implement his vision in public and private schools.

The first primary collaboration in the applied education field between Woodson and African American women was Negro History Week. Widely noted in the relevant scholarly literature, Woodson created "Negro History Week" in 1926.[12] On Woodson's attempt to popularize Negro History, historian Pero Gaglo Dagbovie noted:

> After Woodson founded "Negro History Week" in 1926, black female teachers, club women, librarians, and social activists played essential roles in popularizing the study of Negro history. Without the practical work of women, Woodson's efforts at popularizing African and African American history would not have been nearly as successful. Black women set up activities in schools, such as book displays and pageants; they worked hard to advertise Negro History week celebrations, and they established branches, clubs, and study groups across the country.[13]

The collaboration between Woodson and African American women in the dissemination of Negro History Week reflected the importance of African American women's use of clubs that served as sites for discussion and debates about black history. Consequently, African American women's pre-existing institutional buildings provided the realistic environment in which the African American counter-canon could be implemented, a process well-understood by Woodson.

Woodson created the magazine, *Negro History Bulletin*, to be circulated to primary and secondary teachers. One of the key purposes of the *Negro History Bulletin* was to provide teachers with accurate historical materials for classroom use.[14] As LaGarrett King, Ryan Crowley, and Anthony Brown observed:

> *The Negro History Bulletin* included pages dedicated to current events, poetry, biographical sketches of important black historical figures, primary source documents, plays written by teachers and community members, Negro History Week activities, African knowledge, "Book of the Month" sections and children's pages.[15]

---

[12] Pero Gaglo Dagbovie, "Black Women, Carter G. Woodson, and the Association for the Study of Negro Life and History," 26.

[13] Dagbovie, "Black Women, Carter G. Woodson, and the Association for the Study of Negro Life and History," 30.

[14] LaGarrett J. King, Ryan Crowley, and Anthony L. Brown, "The Forgotten Legacy of Carter G. Woodson: Contributions to Multicultural Social Studies and African American History," 211–215.

[15] King et al, "The Forgotten Legacy," 212.

The April 1939 edition of the *Negro History Bulletin* typified the content that appeared in the publication. The magazine boasted articles on painters Richard Lonsdale Brown, James A. Porter, Aaron Douglas, William H. Johnson, and Palmer Hayden. Short biographies as well as images created by each artist were included. The "Questions of the Month" column got to the heart of the work of the African American counter-canon. In addition to recommending its reader read *To Make a Poet Black*, the editors included questions such as:

1. Trace the place held by the Negro in art from Africa to America.
2. Name at least ten Negro artists.
3. Pay special attention to "Persons and Achievements" to be remembered in March.
4. Contrast the work of Edmonia Lewis with that of Meta Vaux Warrick Fuller.[16]

These prescriptive columns urged the instructor to provide structure for students to use the information in the *Negro History Bulletin* for everyday classroom use.

Other issues of the *Negro History Bulletin* illuminate actual teacher practice. One issue of the *Negro History Bulletin* encouraged black women educators to join in contemporary political debates to exchange "teaching methods" and how to best "incorporate black history into their individual classrooms and their school's curricula." Consequently, the *Negro History Bulletin* needs to be seen as a key liminal text in that it connected the largely female elementary and secondary school educators to the types of teaching materials that would articulate a larger vision for educating African American children. The *Negro History Bulletin* therefore demonstrated that Woodson viewed the teaching of black women with some complexity. While Woodson did not necessarily view black women's scholarship as necessary, Woodson did recognize the professionalization of black women as necessary to the popularization of black history as a discipline.

Notably, Woodson did rely on African American women as he created professional institutions devoted to African American. Mary McLeod Bethune served as the president of the Association for the Study of Negro Life and History (ASNLH) from 1936 to 1952. During her tenure, she

[16] Carter G. Woodson, "The Negro History Bulletin," April 1939.

nurtured the development of the *Negro History Bulletin*.[17] McLeod Bethune also presented scholarly speeches to the larger body of the ASNLH.[18] Carter G. Woodson also worked consistently with Nannie H. Burroughs. He even sent his niece to the National Training School for Women and Girls.[19] Woodson also afforded Burroughs the space to express her ideas about African and African American history. In 1924, Nannie H. Burroughs presented a paper to the Association for the Study of Negro Life and History that extolled virtues of African American ancestry.[20] In 1929, the students from NTS also presented the pageant, *When Truth Gets a Hearing* at the annual meeting of ASNLH. In Woodson and Burroughs's collaboration, we see a deep and reciprocal professional relationship which developed over time.[21]

W.E.B. Du Bois and the Making of the Brownies' Book

W.E.B. Du Bois influenced the development of the alternative black curriculum by writing pageants, publishing *The Crisis* magazine, and collaborating with Jessie Redmon Fauset in the creation of *The Brownies' Book*.

W.E.B. Du Bois viewed the pedagogy of teaching African American children in an expansive fashion. In 1911, he wrote the historical pageant, *The Star of Ethiopia*, which sought to popularize black history.[22] In 1932, W.E.B. Du Bois created *George Washington and Black Folk: A Pageant for the Bicentenary, 1732–1932*, challenging a common trope about American history, the life of George Washington. The pageant focused on black people's contributions during the Federalist Era.

In the 1916 edition of *The Crisis*, Du Bois theorized about the connections between art and black history:

> It seemed to me that it might be possible to get people interested in this development of Negro drama to teach on the one hand the colored people

[17] Dagbovie, "Black Women, Carter G. Woodson, and Association for the Study of Negro Life and History," 30.
[18] Ibid.
[19] Traki Taylor, "Womanhood Glorified", 398.
[20] Dagbovie, "Black Women, Carter G. Woodson, and Association for the Study of Negro Life and History," 30.
[21] Ibid., 31.
[22] James V. Hatch and Ted Shine, eds., *Black Theatre USA: Plays by African-Americans* (New York: The Free Press, 1974), 87.

themselves the meaning of their history and their rich, emotional life through a new theatre, and on the other, to reveal the Negro to the white world as a human feeling thing.[23]

In early editions of *The Crisis*, Du Bois wrote a column entitled, "The Children's Number," which provided young readers poetry, games, photographs, and updates on current events.[24] This interest in working with young people to disseminate African American history and culture led to the creation of *The Brownies' Book* (TBB). Throughout his career, Du Bois sought to align children's literature with Pan-African principles. While Woodson tended to focus on how to navigate the intricacies of segregation within the United States, Du Bois embedded a critique of imperialism and colonialism in his publications, focusing on the working class and the connection with colonial struggles throughout the world.

Du Bois collaborated with Jessie Redmon Fauset, co-editor of *The Crisis*, to create TBB, which was the first literary magazine directed toward African American children.[25] Written in response to the Red Summer of 1919, the editors of the TBB sought to use history and literature to inspire young readers into political action.[26] Much more expansive than the *Negro History Bulletin*, TBB used art and literature to inspire "The Children of the Sun," as the editors affectionately referred to their young readers.[27] *The Brownies' Book* was published from 1920 to 1921, failing after one year because the magazine was too expensive to produce.[28]

The goals of TBB, as articulated by the editors in the first of edition of the magazine were:

1. To make colored children realize that being "colored" is a normal, beautiful, thing.
2. To make them familiar with the history and achievements of the Negro Race.

[23] Hatch and Shine, *Black Theatre USA*, 87.
[24] Courtney Vaughn-Roberson and Brenda Hill, "The Brownies' Book and Ebony Jr.!: Literature as a Mirror of the Afro-American Experience," *The Journal of Negro Education* 58 (Autumn, 1989): 494–510.
[25] Vaughn-Roberson and Hill, "The Brownies' Book," 495.
[26] Katharine Capshaw Smith, *Children's Literature of the Harlem Renaissance* (Bloomington, IN: Indiana University Press, 2004).
[27] Vaughn-Roberson and Hill, "The Brownies' Book," 495.
[28] Ibid., 495.

3. To make them know that other colored children have grown into beautiful, useful, and famous persons.
4. To teach them a delicate code of honor and action in their relations to white children.
5. To turn their little hurts and resentments into emulation, ambition, and love of their homes and companions.
6. To point out the best amusements and joys and worthwhile things of life.
7. To inspire them to prepare for definite occupations and duties with the broad spirit of sacrifice.[29]

In addition, the TBB hoped to counteract negative stereotypes of African American children in literary magazines and textbooks.[30] TBB featured children of the "Talented Tenth," possibly a reason it never became as popular as the *Negro History Bulletin* which was targeted to classroom teachers. The creative flourishing of the Harlem Renaissance heavily influenced the content of *The Brownies' Book*. Historian Viola Harris argued:

> The essence of the Harlem Renaissance pervaded the pages of *The Brownies' Book*. As participants in the movement, Du Bois and Fauset attempted to imbue children with the spirit and substance of the Harlem Renaissance. Arguably, *The Brownies' Book* signaled the creation of an emergent or oppositional tradition imbued with the New Negro philosophy in children's literature.

The content of TBB included short stories and vivid photographs of life in the African American community. It featured columns such as *The Judge* and *As the Crow Flies*. Both Du Bois and Woodson used the developing field of photography to connect visual images of African American vibrancy and pride. Photography and artists' works became extremely important in providing students with visual images of a strong black identity.

Du Bois's work, *As the Crow Flies*, sought to teach his young readers about current events in the United States and in the world. In the third column of *As the Crow Flies*, Du Bois writes in child-friendly language about the financial cost of World War I; starving children in Poland, Serbia, and Russia; the increased rights of the people of India under the British

[29] W.E.B. Du Bois, "The True Brownies," *The Crisis* (1919), 285–286.
[30] Vaughn-Roberson and Hill, "The Brownies' Book," 495.

empire; and the prohibition of alcohol in Norway.[31] The wide-ranging topics in this section attempted to teach children the complexities of world politics. In addition to writing about this variety of topics, Du Bois advocated for the newly emergent political rights of women and reflected on African American participation in world wars.[32] By providing students with an overview of key events in world history, Du Bois sought to encourage black children to be change agents in their communities.

The working relationships between W.E.B. Du Bois and women were markedly different than those of Woodson. Woodson worked with women educators far more frequently than Du Bois because of the Association of Negro Life and History's constant promotion of black history. W.E.B. Du Bois, on the other hand, advanced a more pro-feminist agenda in his academic writings and essays.[33] In his writings he emphasized the political rights of women and exulted the critical role women played in rebuilding the black community at the end of the Civil War. However, promoting the rights of women did not necessarily mean recognizing them as fellow academics. Joy James theorized:

> Quoting Anna Julia Cooper's now-famous, "When and where I enter" sentence in "Damnation of Women," Du Bois fails to mention her by name, prefacing his remarks with the proprietary phrase: "As one of our women writes." Du Bois' selective questions curtail Cooper's full argument; the passage preceding the quote more accurately reflects the critical mandate for black leadership echoing throughout *A Voice from the South*.[34]

The obscuring of women's work is typified in Du Bois' collaboration with Jessie Redmon Fauset. W.E.B. Du Bois often took public credit for the creation and the conception of TBB, whereas it was Fauset who had taken a very active role in conceptualizing the approach and pedagogy of TBB.

Jessie Redmon Fauset served as a collaborator in the development of the alternative black curriculum. A former librarian, she is often described

---

[31] W.E.B. Du Bois, "As the Crow Flies" *The Brownies' Book*, 1920, V2.

[32] Viola J. Harris, "Race Consciousness, Refinement, and Radicalism: Socialization in The Brownies' Book," *Children's Literature Association Quarterly* 14 (1989): 195.

[33] Joy James, *Transcending the Talented Tenth: Black Leaders and American Intellectuals* (New York: Routledge, 1997), 43.

[34] Joy James, *Transcending the Talented Tenth*, 44.

as a "literary" midwife in the blossoming of the Harlem Renaissance.[35] She encouraged the poetry of young black writers such as Langston Hughes whose first published poem, "A Negro Speaks Rivers," appeared in *The Crisis*.[36] Although her work tended to exemplify upper middle-class black mores, Fauset represented a different type of elite black activist woman. Deeply enmeshed in the literary scene of New York, she allied herself philosophically with the "New Negro" movement which permeated the black community in the 1920s. With her immersion in the art scene, she authored four books: *There is Confusion* (1932), *Plum Bun* (1929), *The Chinaberry Tree* (1931), and *Comedy: American Style* (1933), contributing significantly to the literature during the period.[37]

As the literary editor of *The Crisis*, Fauset collaborated with Du Bois and shared in the development of the alternative black curriculum. From 1919 to 1926, she served as the co-editor of *The Crisis*. As co-editor of *The Crisis* and TBB, Fauset advocated for the use of biography to extend children's understanding of black history. Abby Arthur Johnson described Fauset's commitment to biography in stating:

> While literary editor, Fauset also contributed informative essays to The Crisis. She especially favored biographical sketches of blacks prominent in her day and in the past. Among others, she wrote about Jose Don Patrocino, who fought for the "abolition of slavery in Brazil"; Robert Brown Elliott, who represented a South Carolina district in the forty-second and forty-third Congresses of the United States; and Henry Ossawa Turner, prominent artist. She found Bert Williams an appealing subject because he, as a comedian, "symbolized that deep, ineluctable strain of melancholy, which no Negro in a mixed civilization ever lacks.[38]

She felt that the use of biography would uplift and inspire African American children to achieve great accomplishments in their larger community. Fauset also shared Du Bois's belief that African American children needed to be aware and involved in struggles for freedom across the Caribbean, Latin America, and Africa.

---

[35] Abby Arthur Johnson, "Literary Midwife: Jessie Redmon Fauset and the Harlem Renaissance," *Phylon* (1978): 145.
[36] Carolyn Wedin Sylvander, *Jessie Redmon Fauset, Black American Writer* (Troy, NY: The Whitson Publishing Company, 1981), 116.
[37] Johnson, "Literary Midwife," 143.
[38] Johnson, "Literary Midwife," 147.

So, while Carter G. Woodson shaped children's historical memories using a factual narrative, W.E.B. Du Bois fashioned a historical narrative that was heavily influenced by his passion and love for the arts.

Changing the Narrative and the African American Counter-Canon

Changing the narrative was a deliberate strategy in building the African American canon. As discussed, the dominant narrative of African Americans' invisibility in building the country, and more perniciously, the inability of African Americans to participate as full citizens after Reconstruction. This dominant narrative was pervasive as it was reinforced in public spaces such as schools and museums, and in private spaces through family stories and novels.

Challenging this dominant narrative was quite difficult, particularly given the limited resources that confronted African American scholars both in relationship to institution building and their individual resources. Reconstruction of the African American counter-canon calls for new ways of telling the story given the frequent professional and personal "silences" imposed on African Americans during this period. This section looks at two categories of work to tell the story of the content of the African American counter-canon. First, a group biography approach is used to see how African American women used various strategies to reframe the dominant narrative behind mainstream curriculum. Finally, an examination of the two major academic works of the African American canon, *The Mis-Education of the Negro*, and *Black Reconstruction* is conducted.

Collaborations between African American male academics and African American women often occurred along lines of subordination insofar as the relationships reflected standard gender relationships between men and women in the early twentieth century. African American women, however, played a key role in creating the new counter-canon, but a new approach is necessary to highlight their work. While the scholarly literature has addressed the work of women such as Leila Amos Pendleton, Elizabeth Ross Haynes, and Laura Wilkes individually, it is when we examine their work collectively in diverse forms such as textbooks, historical fiction, and monographs that we see how the African American attempted to reframe an often inaccurate "master narrative."

Leila Amos Pendleton

Of the three women discussed in this Chapter, the scholarly literature on Leila Amos Pendleton is the most illuminating. LaGarrett King's article, "A Narrative to the Colored Children in America: Leila Amos Pendleton, African American History Textbooks, and Challenging Personhood," is the seminal article focused on her work in the field of education. King's treatment of Leila Amos Pendleton correctly establishes her role of a key architect of the African American counter-canon given the scope of her work in this area.

A few basic facts can be established based on the sparse biographical information available. Leila Amos Pendleton was born in 1860 in Washington, DC, a daughter of a policeman who served the Washington, DC community. She received her education at the Washington High School (1886) and subsequently graduated from Minor Normal School which focused on preparing students for teaching careers. Leila Amos Pendleton specialized in English during her time at the normal school and then taught for four years until marrying Robert Pendleton in 1893. Robert Pendleton offered a key resource to Leila Amos Pendleton as he owned a printing house that was sometimes referred to as Pendleton's Quality Printing House or Pendleton's Printing House, depending on the source.[39] Leila Pendleton did not have an extensive professional career, unlike other female authors of the counter-canon. Yet, despite her limited professional career, Leila Pendleton became one of the most prolific black social studies writers of her era.

Two tentative conclusions can be reached from this biographical information. First, Leila Pendleton participated extensively in the type of institutional resources that Carter Woodson used to popularize the counter-canon. Leila Pendleton's community involvement included being the first vice president of the Northeast Federation of the Women's Club and a member of the National Association of Colored Women's Clubs and serving as the founder and president of the Alpha Charity Club. Leila Pendleton was clearly enmeshed in the types of activities that would have led her to be interested in creating texts that uplifted and celebrated the black child. Second, Leila Amos Pendleton could rely on

---

[39] LaGarrett King, "A Narrative to the Colored Children in America": Leila Amos Pendleton, African American History, Textbooks, and Challenging Personhood," *The Journal of Negro Education* 84 (4), 519–533.

her marital relationship with Robert Pendleton, which permitted her to publish at rate that was not available to other African American women of her era. Leila Amos Pendleton published at least three books through Pendleton's Quality Printing House including *A Narrative of the Negro* (1912), *An Alphabet for Negro Children (1915)*, and *Frederick Douglass, A Narrative* (1921). Outside of her husband's support, Leila Pendleton also published *Our New Possessions-The Danish West Indies,* an article which appeared in the *Journal of Negro History* in 1917. Finally, Leila Amos Pendleton also wrote a series of short stories that appeared in *The Crisis* during the Harlem Renaissance.[40]

The consistency and breadth of Leila Pendleton's work is significant, and it suggests that she had considerable autonomy due to her relationship with Robert Pendleton. The body of work produced by Leila Amos Pendleton is also notable as it ranged from non-fiction work in educational texts to short stories.

A Narrative of the Negro

One of the earliest texts in the development of the counter-canon in social studies is Leila Amos Pendleton's book, *A Narrative of the Negro*, written in 1912. Indeed, *A Narrative of the Negro* appeared before *The Negro* written by W.E.B. Du Bois in 1915 as well as other works important to the development of the alternative black curriculum.

A Narrative of the Negro establishes several strategies associated with the African American counter-canon. Initially, Leila Amos Pendleton establishes an affirmative claim that her readership of African American children deserved to receive information in an affirmative, caring manner. Early in the book she established that this work was attempting to strengthen the love black children should have for the continent of Africa, a theme echoed by other authors of the counter-canon. Additionally, Leila Amos Pendleton exhorted to students to also take pride in being Black. Establishing that African American children deserved to read material that affirmed their self-identity speaks to how the counter-canon attempted to shape a landscape of resistance. *A Narrative of the Negro* is, therefore, grounded in a sense of pride in the legitimacy and value of the African American experience.

[40] LaGarrett King, *A Narrative to the Colored Children in America*, 521.

The African American counter-canon is also grounded in specific content techniques. Throughout *A Narrative of the Negro*, Ms. Pendleton used a regional approach to explore the key components of world history. Specifically, Leila Amos Pendleton claimed that African geography played an important role in world history:

> Let us look at a map of the Eastern Hemisphere. In the northern part we see Europe and Asia, and southwest of these lies Africa, almost entirely in the Torrid Zone...Remember these countries, for on their soil many of the most important events of the ancient world took place. Some hundreds of years before our Savior was born in Bethlehem, hundreds of years before men had even heard the names "England," "France," "Germany," "America," the people of northern Africa were engaged in building cities, sailing the waters, and rearing statues and monuments, some of which latter are standing until this day.[41]

Two key elements of the African American counter-canon are clear from this passage. First, the African American counter-canon centered the continent of Africa as pivotal in world history. Leila Amos Pendleton posited that the kingdoms of Abyssinia and Meroe were as influential as Rome or Greece. Moreover, Pendleton interspersed a variety of illustrations to support and supplement the narrative throughout her entire book. For instance, in the section on Ancient Africa, Pendleton used a map of Africa and an image of Meroe to augment her analysis. This positive emphasis on the achievements of Africa attempted to counter the dominant narrative's emphasis on African inferiority. Second, Pendleton tried to shape black children's identity in a positive way by using a warm, inclusive "we."

Pendleton, as an element of creation of the counter-canon, also attempted to reframe the dominant narrative around then debate over the usefulness of colonization. For instance, in *A Narrative of the Negro*, Pendleton described the journeys of Mungo Park, a native of Scotland, through West Africa in the eighteenth century, as well as describing the colonization of Sierra Leone and Liberia.[42] To support her claim, Pendleton used imagery effectively, including the pictures "A Native Youth of Modern Africa," "Image of the Native King and Council, Hinterland Sierra Leone,"

---

[41] Leila Amos Pendleton, *A Narrative of the Negro* (Washington, DC: Press of R.L. Pendleton, 1915), 9.
[42] Pendleton, *A Narrative of the Negro*, 38–44.

and "Image of Liberian Soldiers and Citizens."[43] Pendleton's rewriting of the history of colonization is a set of complex choices. It appears that central to her understanding of the counter-canon was her attempt to place colonization into a larger history of Christianity; hence the centrality of Sierra Leone and Liberia in her story. Pendleton's language, however, often seems paternalistic in her discussion of the ways in which the colonies of Sierra Leone and Liberia were functioning in the twentieth century.

A Narrative of the Negro is also notable in its emphasis on understanding the struggle of African Americans in a diasporic context. After discussing colonization, Pendleton described the freedom struggles in Santo Domingo/Haiti. The centrality of Haitian Revolution in the alternative black curriculum in social studies cannot be overstated. Toussaint L'Ouverture could be juxtaposed with George Washington, thus providing the counter-canon with its own mythos. Moreover, Haiti provided figures like Pendleton, with a way to discuss black freedom and autonomy, an important counter-narrative to the dominant narrative of inferiority. Pendleton extended this claim to a discussion of a free black maroon community in Brazil and Haiti.[44]

Another key element of this diasporic claim was Pendleton's attempt to reframe the conversation about slavery. Pendleton attempted to enumerate the types of slavery throughout world history, noting that the phenomenon of slavery was not a political condition found only in the United States. This perceived effort to normalize the conditions of African Americans may have underplayed the extent to which modern slavery, with its reliance on networks of capitalism, was truly different historical phenomena. Pendleton's discussion of slavery, perhaps not always successful in its content analysis, once again employed her use of empathy as strategy to aid her young readers in understanding the condition of slavery. Notably, in an effort to connect with her audience of grade level children, Pendleton opened the chapter using the rearing of a kitten as a metaphor for slavery.[45]

Finally, Pendleton moved on to the history of the United States. As she transitioned from world and diasporic history, Pendleton uncovered another key element of the counter-canon—the centrality of the African American citizenship to the history of the United States. In her treatment

---

[43] Pendleton, *A Narrative of the Negro*, 44–53.
[44] Pendleton, *A Narrative of the Negro*, 54–63.
[45] Pendleton, *A Narrative of the Negro*, 74–80.

of the early colonial period, Pendleton emphasized the Negro Plot of 1741, a plot between blacks and poor whites to burn New York City by setting a series of fires, and the role of Jenny Slew, one of the first black women to sue for freedom against her master to decenter the colonial experience. Through this decentering, Pendleton elucidated the origins of African American citizenship.[46] This decentering of citizenship continued, as Pendleton developed another common theme essential to the alternative black curriculum in social studies—the role of the black man in the military of the United States. Pendleton equated military service with citizenship as she discussed the role of Crispus Attucks and other black men during the Revolutionary War, the military service of African American sailors during the War of 1812, and the impact of black soldiers in the Civil War.[47]

These stories asserted black manhood and, by extension, black citizenship in the face of endemic racism. Pendleton complicated this story by extending her discussion to illuminate the black participants in the Harpers Ferry Raid, recognizing that:

> In the little burial ground of Oberlin, Lorain County, Ohio, there is a monument dedicated to the memory of three of John Brown's men as follows:
> L.S. Leary, died at Harper's Ferry, October 20, 1859, aged twenty-four.
> S. Green, died at Charlestown Va., December 2, 1859, aged twenty-eight years.
> J.A. Copeland, died at Charlestown Va. December 2, 1859, aged twenty-five years.
> These colored citizens of Oberlin, the heroic associates of the immortal John Brown, gave their lives for the slave.[48]

With this, Pendleton engaged in a sophisticated rereading of the narrative that equated black military service in the official military as being necessary for citizenship. Rather, for Pendleton, her reference to the memorial granted to citizenship to those men, whose service was linked to larger discussions of freedom.

---

[46] Pendleton, *A Narrative of the Negro*, 83.
[47] Pendleton, *A Narrative of the Negro*, 101.
[48] Pendleton, *A Narrative of the Negro*, 156.

Finally, Pendleton stressed the accomplishments of African American women. She placed the experiences of African American women in the center of the counter-canon. Indeed, in this element, *A Narrative of the Negro* creates a mythos of black womanhood that Pendleton uses to reframe the current institutional structures of the Progressive Era with black female figures equivalent to those mythical figures of George Washington and Thomas Jefferson at the center of the dominant narrative. Pendleton devoted an entire chapter to Phillis Wheatley and discussed at equal length, Sojourner Truth, Harriet Tubman, and Frances Ellen Harper. Pendleton then extends this mythos of citizenship to the current clubwomen such as of Fanny Jackson Coppin and the growing role of the black women's club movement. This became a narrative to help socialize black women into a claim of citizenship that was equal to those of black men.[49]

Thus, as early as 1912, key elements of the counter-canon are present in *A Narrative of the Negro*. The first innovation, a modeling of African American teaching that built on empathetic understanding of the student, was, of course, simply a technique. This technique, however, is most likely the most revolutionary aspect of *A Narrative of the Negro*, because it presumed that the African American student was one that deserves empathy on the part of the teacher as a matter of course. Other innovations included the decentering of a Eurocentric geography, the disruption of simple colonization narratives, and the reclamation of citizenship for African American men and women. The importance of Pendleton to building the counter-canon, therefore, cannot be underestimated.

Acknowledging this importance does not mean that *A Narrative of the Negro* is without flaws. Initially, *A Narrative of the Negro* is exactly that—a narrative. Pendleton did not reflect the professional norms of history insofar as she did not use citations throughout the book, or use transparent notation. Moreover, *A Narrative of the Negro* contains key factual errors. For example, she referred to Deborah Sampson, a white woman who fought in the American Revolution, as a black woman.[50] Consequently, *A Narrative of the Negro* is not often referred to in discussions of a broader social curriculum. *A Narrative of the Negro* deserves more attention, both for its usefulness in outlining the parameters of the African American canon and the basic fact that the book's existence reflects that Pendleton published during an era which was constricted by the unyielding bonds of sexism and racism.

[49] Pendleton, *A Narrative of the Negro*, 139–142.
[50] Pendleton, *A Narrative of the Negro*, 101.

ELIZABETH ROSS HAYNES

Elizabeth Ross Haynes was born on July 30, 1883 to an Alabama family with considerable wealth. She attended the State Normal School in Montgomery, Alabama, then Fisk University in Nashville where she was awarded an AB in 1903. Like her contemporaries, Haynes taught school for a period of six years, and then turned toward social work at the Student Department of the National Board of the YWCA in New York. While in New York, Haynes married George Edmund Haynes, the co-founder and first executive of the National Urban League. After her marriage, Mrs. Ross Haynes never returned to teaching. Like Pendleton, Haynes' middle-class status permitted her to refrain from teaching in public schools.[51] Despite her decision to refrain from teaching, Haynes remained a professional, serving as a domestic service employment secretary from 1920 to 1922. In that capacity, she wrote *Two Million Negroes at Work*, a monograph which outlined conditions for black women in domestic service and which remains her most well-recognized work.[52] In 1923, Haynes pursued a master's degree in political science and sociology at Columbia University and published a thesis that also focused on the employment conditions for black women in domestic service. Additionally, Haynes served as a member of the National Association of Colored Women (NACW), the Harlem Branch of the YWCA, and the Mary F. Waring Club. Haynes was active in politics as the co-leader of Harlem's Twenty-first Assembly District. Haynes' employment and civic activism, once again, tied her to the institutional structure of the counter-canon.[53]

Elizabeth Haynes's intellectual contribution to the African American counter-canon includes two books, *Unsung Heroes* (1921) and *The Black Boy of Atlanta* (1952). *Unsung Heroes* is a work of historical fiction written in biographical form directed to students between 9 and 15. She selected the following figures to highlight in the book: Frederick Douglass, Paul Laurence Dunbar, Booker T. Washington, Harriet Tubman, Alexander S. Pushkin, Blanche Kelso Bruce, Samuel Coleridge-Taylor, Benjamin Banneker, Phillis Wheatley, Toussaint L'Ouverture, Josiah Henson, Sojourner Truth, Crispus Attucks, Paul Cuffee, Alexander Crummell, and John Mercer Langston.[54]

---

[51] Iris Carlton-LaNey, "Elizabeth Ross Haynes: An African American Reformer of Womanist Consciousness, 1908–1940," *Social Work* 42(6), 573–583.

[52] Carlton-LaNey, *Elizabeth Ross Haynes*, 577.

[53] Carlton-LaNey, *Elizabeth Ross Haynes*, 578.

[54] Elizabeth Ross Haynes, *Unsung Heroes* (New York: Du Bois and Dill, Publishers, 1921).

Introducing each chapter of *Unsung Heroes*, Haynes begins with a vignette of the hero and heroines as children. For example, in her vignette of Frederick Douglass, Haynes emphasizes Douglass's relationship with his grandmother.[55] Haynes, as Pendleton, thus is relying on the technique of empathy, insofar as the book encourages young students to empathize with the named heroes.[56] Interestingly, Haynes simultaneously projects the mythos of the counter-canon while also attempting to encourage her readers to see these figures as human.

Haynes also used other techniques of the counter-canon. First, *Unsung Heroes* situates Africa as pivotal to her reader's identities. Throughout the book Haynes invokes the metaphor of Ethiopia, a non-colonized, nominally Christian country, to explain the relationship of Africa to her reader's political identities. Second, *Unsung Heroes* invokes diasporic identity by introducing figures such as Alexandre Dumas, Paul Cuffee, and Alexandre Crummell. These figures, Haynes suggests, reflect the complex racial backgrounds of black people across the diaspora. Haynes also focused in on questions of multiracial identity and citizenship. Haynes sought to complicate binary social identities by embracing the lived experiences of black men who interacted with European countries such as Great Britain, France, and Russia. For Haynes, these biographies illustrated that race was a mutable concept within political democracies. Finally, throughout *Unsung Heroes*, Haynes countered the dominant narrative by focusing on the roles African Americans played in shaping politics in the United States, writing about political figures John Langston Mercer and Blanche Kelso Bruce during the Reconstruction period.[57] Notably, in her introductory vignette of Blanche Kelso Bruce, she also illuminated the importance of white allies as she reflected on Bruce's relationship with Roscoe Conkling. In this way, Haynes could stress to her reader that multiracial democratic politics was a reality.

Haynes's work, however, innovative, still had significant conceptual limits. *Unsung Heroes* is dominated by male figures unlike, for instance, the historical pageant whose authors tended to try to include references to female figures. Beyond the dominance of male historical figures, Haynes also failed to include female figures other than Harriet Tubman, Phillis Wheatley, and Sojourner Truth. Despite this failure of inclusivity,

[55] Ross Haynes, *Unsung Heroes*, 11.
[56] Ibid., 41.
[57] Ibid., 117.

her description of each women's life focused on biographical details that often went unnoticed. In her chapter on Harriet Tubman, Haynes acknowledged Tubman's role in the Underground Railroad and also delved into Tubman's activism in advocating for indigent elderly people in upstate New York.[58] Likewise, in her discussion of Sojourner Truth, Haynes highlighted Truth's participation in the Great Second Awakening along with her more famous speeches, such as "Ain't I a Woman."[59] In doing so, Haynes, once again, adds complexity to the mythos of the counter-canon.

Laura Eliza Wilkes

Laura Eliza Wilkes, the final author considered in this chapter, contains the least documented biographical traces. Wilkes was born in 1871 and graduated from the Normal High School in Washington, DC. She taught first in Winston, North Carolina, and later in Washington, DC. Traces of Laura Eliza Wilkes' public career come from her two books, *Missing Pages in American History: Revealing the Services of Negroes, in the Early Wars in the United States*, published in 1919, and *The Story of Frederick Douglass, with quotations*, published in 1899. In *Missing Pages*, Wilkes proudly identified herself as a classroom teacher.[60] We also know that her books were published by R.L. Pendleton Books, a direct connection to Leila Amos Pendleton, and this suggests institutional structures like publishing companies also served to reinforce the emerging counter-canon.

Missing Pages seems to be a prototypical counter-canon text. Wilkes claimed a diasporic identity central to the counter-canon first by analyzing the importance of the Haitian Revolution during the Revolutionary Era as central turning point in the establishment of a political African American life. She coupled this with a complex story of the War of 1812, amidst the emancipatory possibilities signaled by a growing free black population.[61]

Second, *Missing Pages* links the military service of African Americans to overall claims of citizenship. Wilkes exhaustively listed evidence that

---

[58] Ibid., 87.
[59] Ibid., 209.
[60] Laura E. Wilkes, *Missing Pages in American History: Revealing the Services of Negroes in the Early Wars in the United States of America, 1614–1815* (London: Forgotten Books, 2015).
[61] Wilkes, *Missing Pages in American History: Revealing the Services of Negroes in the Early Wars in the United States of America, 1614–1815*, 56.

African Americans participated in every military conflict from the colonial period. Wilkes first discussed the participation of African American slaves in warding off advances by American Indians, both informally and formally, in the French and Indian War.[62] Wilkes then examined the experience of African Americans in the American Revolution. She provided detailed accounts of African American contributions to the war effort in 13 colonies. She referenced Salem of New York, Prince Whipple, and the countless other black men who fought for freedom during the American Revolution. Moreover, as she discussed the American Revolution in the South, she outlined Lord Dunmore's Proclamation that slaves who had fought for the British could obtain freedom.[63] If one examines American textbooks, there is typically a section on how blacks navigated British and American desires for how they would use slaves.

Wilkes's explicit recitation of bravery is a way of invoking citizenship, making the claim that African Americans are deserving of citizenship if military service to the country is what produces citizenship. Additionally, through her complex examination of the colonial and revolutionary period, Wilkes situated the early struggles for freedom in the North as much as in the South, thus challenging the dominative narrative that racism was a product of the traditional society in the South. Specifically, Wilkes claimed that the history of black service in the American Revolution was among the reasons why gradual emancipation emerged after the Revolution in most of the Northern states. Finally, Wilkes grappled with the mythos of the canon, by stressing that the acts of "ordinary" black men were as relevant to the approved pantheon of influences in American history.

Missing Pages, though, maintains an interesting place in the emerging counter-canon. First, unlike the work of Pendleton and Haynes, Wilkes aligned her practices in *Missing Pages* with professional historical methods in the opening paragraph for her monograph. She emphasized that in the course of her research, she reviewed "colonial records, state papers, assembly journals, histories of slavery and old-time histories of the various colonies."[64] *Missing Pages* contains a well-sourced bibliography. Second, unlike Pendleton and Haynes, Wilkes never offered a critique of patriarchy in any material manner. *Missing Pages* is a narrative about men, military

[62] Ibid., 17.
[63] Ibid., 26–30.
[64] Ibid., 5.

service, and citizenship; it ends with the famous Battle of New Orleans where she explored the relationship between black soldiers and Andrew Jackson.[65] Finally, unlike the works of Pendleton and Haynes, *Missing Pages* contains racist language directed at Native Americans, referring to them as "murderous" and "redskins."[66] In this sense, Wilkes deviated from the empathetic content of the counter-canon.

FOUNDATIONAL TEXTS IN THE COUNTER-CANON

The works of Pendleton, Haynes, and Wilkes set the parameters for the articulation of the counter-canon. The counter-canon, as noted previously, used rhetorical techniques such as empathetic outreach to the reader, as well as informational challenges to the primary claims of the dominant narrative. The counter-canon, therefore, served as a key response to the dominant narrative in the social studies curriculum. However, if modern scholarship has grappled with the counter-canon, two works are seen to be been at the core of the counter-canon: *The Mis-Education of the Negro* and *Black Reconstruction*.

The publications *The Mis-Education of the Negro* (1933) and *Black Reconstruction* (1935) introduced fundamental frameworks that improved scholarly understandings of black people and challenged traditional historiography. Furthermore, Woodson and Jesse E. Moorland also founded the *Journal of Negro History* as a venue for the publication of black history, often excluded from mainstream historical journals such as the *Journal of American History*. Both Woodson and Du Bois generated innovative epistemological frameworks about the experience of African Americans in the United States. This section will consider *The Mis-Education of the Negro* and *Black Reconstruction*, in turn.

The Mis-education of the Negro and Black Reconstruction

In 1933, Carter G. Woodson published *The Mis-Education of Negro*.[67] This book analyzed how to repair a fragile education system that developed in the South after the end of the Civil War. Woodson argued that African Americans received an impoverished education in the newly

---

[65] Ibid., 76–84.
[66] Ibid.
[67] Ibid.

established schools in the South because of the lack of economic resources provided by white school boards. Woodson further believed that the education students were receiving was at best, incomplete and at worst, dehumanizing. Jeffrey Aaron Snyder recently placed *The Mis-Education of the Negro* squarely in a Progressive Era tradition of education. In a comprehensive argument Snyder surmised that Woodson believed that the central purpose of education was to be relevant to the lives of students.[68] By introducing one of the central tenants of the alternative black curriculum, Woodson rejected the purpose of the missionary education and the controlling nature of historically black colleges and universities. Heavily influenced by his experiences teaching in the Philippines, Woodson argued that schools must address "those objects, songs and stories from their immediate environment."[69]

Woodson argued that the discipline of history was especially critical to the development and empowerment of African American children. He believed that in order to combat educational racism, fundamental changes needed to occur in how literature, math, science, and history were taught. Woodson also advocated for more engaging instruction to motivate students.[70] In his analysis of the structural deficits of African American education, Woodson constructed a conceptual framework of an alternative black curriculum. In the chapter entitled, "The New Program," Woodson articulates his vision of the purposes of history:

> The leading facts of history of the world should be studied by all, but what advantage is it to the Negro student of history to devote all of his time to courses bearing on such despots as Alexander the Great, Caesar, and Napoleon, or to the record of those natives whose outstanding achievement has been rapine, plunder and murder for world power? Why not study the African background from the point of view of anthropology and history, and then take up sociology as it concerns the Negro peasant or proletarian who is suffering from sufficient ills to supply laboratory work for the most advanced students of the social order.[71]

In the *Mis-Education of the Negro*, Woodson articulated a series of principles that would become the framework for the alternative black curricu-

---

[68] Jeffrey Aaron Snyder, "Progressive Education in Black and White," 273–293.
[69] Snyder, "Progressive Education," 280.
[70] Carter G. Woodson, *The Mis-Education of the Negro*, 1–8.
[71] Woodson, *The Mis-Education of the Negro*, 150.

lum. A critical component to this idea was that to be educated, African Americans needed to create a framework that directly challenged European hegemonic discourse. The basic principles of the alternative black curriculum articulated in *The Mis-Education of the Negro* included:

1. a counter-response that stressed the importance of African civilizations such as Abyssinia, Nubia, Kush, Mali, and Ghana[72]
2. a counter-response that stressed the importance of African American contributions, such as the value of slave labor in building the key infrastructure of the early United States[73]
3. a recognition for the role Africans and African Americans have played in shaping the political culture of the United States—African American educators of Woodson's time argued that the voices of Harriet Tubman, Frederick Douglass, and other key black leaders should be studied along with the "Founding Fathers"[74]
4. a defense of black labor—scholars wanted to acknowledge the tradition of entrepreneurship in the black community[75]
5. a Pan-African vision which linked African American struggles with the struggles of people of color from other parts of the world—African American activists stressed the role of the Haitian Revolution in shaping a black identity in the Western Hemisphere
6. an inclusion of stories of resistance and rebellion to slavery[76]
7. a discussion about the impact of race and racism[77]
8. an inclusion of white allies in the struggle against racism

The principles articulated by Woodson were echoed in the scholarship being produced by other black academics in the early twentieth century.[78]

W.E.B. Du Bois played a significant role in the creation of the alternative black curriculum by crafting a response to white historical scholars in the early twentieth century. However, while crafting an approach to black history in the United States, he also included an international dimension

[72] Ibid., 19.
[73] Ibid., 7.
[74] Ibid., 18.
[75] Ibid., 21.
[76] Brown, "Counter-memory and Race," 62.
[77] Jeffrey Aaron Snyder, "Race, Nation and Education," 86.
[78] These scholars included W.E.B. Du Bois, Rayford Logan, Charles Wesley, Lorenzo Green, and Anna Julia Cooper.

to his scholarship. Du Bois created a significant body of scholarly work before authoring *Black Reconstruction*. His earlier works included his doctoral dissertation at Harvard, *The Suppression of the African Slave Trade in the United States, 1638–1870* (1896); *The Souls of Black Folks* (1903); *John Brown*; (1909); *The Quest for the Silver Fleece* (1911); and *The Negro* (1915). *Black Reconstruction* became such an important text because it rebutted one of the key historical schools of thought at the turn of the twentieth century, the Dunning School of Reconstruction. In addition, Du Bois created a method of analysis which demonstrated how scholars of color could question intellectual myths and misconceptions about people of color.

The subversive nature of *Black Reconstruction* emerges immediately in the first chapter of the book as Du Bois discussed the history of African Americans in the United States. Chapter 2, entitled "The Black Worker," placed African Americans as central actors in the sweep of history. One of the key ideas of the alternative black curriculum is the belief that African Americans should be placed at the center of their own history. Throughout the remainder of the book, Du Bois used an objective collection of data which mirrors the methodological approach of white historians.

Whereas Woodson attempted to create a history for the masses, Du Bois targeted a very specific and elite audience of white historians. Another example of Du Bois's reexamination of the Reconstruction period occurred in his discussion of the growth of public schools in the South. Du Bois persuasively argued that the growth of public schools was the "crowning achievement" of the Reconstruction period.[79] Once again, Du Bois characterized African Americans as possessing agency in history, which was unusual for history written during that period.

Beyond issues of content, scholars of the alternative black curriculum addressed epistemological concerns. Du Bois's final chapter offered a stinging critique of the historiography of Reconstruction. In the chapter entitled, "The Propaganda of History," Du Bois argued that the work of John Burgess and William Dunning was incorrect and riddled with misconceptions.[80] Du Bois critiqued the methodology of the Reconstruction historians because their primary sources did not include the range of primary sources authored by and about African Americans that were available to them. While Woodson was interested in lambasting key figures in the black community, Du Bois pointed his arguments toward white historians.

[79] Du Bois, *Black Reconstruction*, 667.
[80] Ibid., 718.

This type of rhetorical uncovering of misinformation is central to the alternative black curriculum. While white scholars collaborated in largely segregated environments, black scholars were creating their own curriculum which invoked a profoundly different understanding of major events in US and world history.[81]

Much like Woodson, Du Bois directly attacked the commonly taught narratives in the nation's social studies classrooms. Du Bois posited that in high school classes, African Americans, during the period of Reconstruction, were framed in one of four ways. Du Bois argued that African Americans were portrayed as "ignorant," "lazy," "dishonest," or "extravagant."[82] In addition, Du Bois believed that most teachers portrayed African Americans as "responsible for bad government during the Reconstruction period."[83] Furthermore, Du Bois attacked the role of textbooks in the social studies classroom stating:

> Grounded in such elementary and high school teaching, an American youth attending college today would learn from current textbooks of history that the Constitution recognized slavery; that the chance of getting rid of slavery by peaceful methods was ruined by the Abolitionists; that after the period of Andrew Jackson, the two sections of the United States "had become fully conscious of their conflicting interests. Two irreconcilable forms of civilization…in the North, the democratic….in the South, a more stationary and aristocratic civilization.[84]

Du Bois recognized and understood the power of stories, a feature that critical race theory today also affirms. He understood intimately that the story being told by teachers in the K-12 environment influenced students about the role African Americans played in US history.

Conclusion

It is important to ask why works such as *A Narrative of a Negro*, *Unsung Heroes*, and *Missing Pages* have been ignored if such works predated *The Mis-Education of the Negro* and *Black Reconstruction*. The simplest explanation is often the best explanation. Pendleton's, Wilkes's, and Haynes's gender is likely the primary culprit considering that gender shaped the

---

[81] Ibid.
[82] Du Bois, *Black Reconstruction*, 712.
[83] Ibid.
[84] Ibid., 713.

opportunities for those women in building the type of audience that would consistently invest in their works as intellectuals. Second, Pendleton and Haynes's works could have been seen as extensions of their "womanly" identity that were reinforced through structures, rather than a fully independent identity of an author. Finally, the way in which Pendleton, Haynes, and Wilkes experimented with the "form" of historical material rather than through a "scholarly" monograph perhaps made it likely that this was not work considered to be part of a mainstream historical method. This experimentation with form likely furthered the distance between acceptable treatments and what would become unacceptable forms of the counter-canons—the invisible work of the female innovators of the counter-canon.

CHAPTER 5

Exploring the Purposes and Foundations of Black Teacher Preparation: 1890–1940

The alternative black curriculum, in part, emerged out of new methods of social studies teacher training. In its different elements, the alternative black curriculum engaged extensively in reconsidering techniques that would effectively impact the educational lives of black students. As noted throughout the book, black women had the most freedom and impact in the K-12 arena. Research about women's roles in and impact on higher education policy conversations about teacher preparation and education is limited. Thus, this chapter will focus primarily on the contributions of Carter G. Woodson and Booker T. Washington in their discussions about how to best prepare teachers for their work in elementary and secondary schools.

This chapter examines how the alternative black curriculum impacted teaching training during the relevant era, 1900–1920. Three interrelated subjects will be considered: first, the primary models of teaching training in the Post-Reconstruction Era; second, new models of teaching training that emerged during the Progressive Era; and finally, how scholars in teaching training attempted to adjust to the emerging alternative black curriculum.

© The Author(s) 2018
A. D. Murray, *The Development of the Alternative Black Curriculum, 1890–1940*,
https://doi.org/10.1007/978-3-319-91418-3_5

Teaching Training in the Post-Reconstruction Era

The legal, social, and political constraints on African American education prior to Reconstruction are well known. Historian Heather Andrea Williams's, *Self-Taught: African American Education in Slavery and Freedom*, emphasizes the formal and informal networks that attempted to overcome significant barriers to literacy (for instance, the fact that by the 1820s, Southern states made it gradually more difficulty to learn the skills of literacy).[1] Consequently, after Reconstruction, access to basic literacy became a significant goal for newly freed slaves because it guaranteed access to economic and social power.

The politics of literacy during the Post-Reconstruction Era were quite complex. As David Tyack and Robert Lowe have noted:

> Public education was a central concern of those Radical Republican lawmakers who sought to bring about a republican political order that would include blacks as full citizens.[2]

The structure of African American education, therefore, became a fraught battle. Two debates occurred during the era that were specific to teacher training. The first centered around whether African Americans should be the primary educators of African American children. The second debate occurred over the type of curriculum that would be offered to African American teachers in teaching preparation programs. These debates were linked to larger questions of what the purposes of educating African Americans should be after the experience of enslavement.

Who Should Teach? Citizenship, Preparation, and the African American Educator in Reconstruction Era

The politics of education in the Post-Reconstruction Era were driven by significantly differing goals. Northern missionaries, Southern politicians, black leaders, black parents, and even black students themselves participated

---

[1] Heather Andrea Williams, *Self-Taught: African American Education in Slavery and Freedom* (Chapel Hill: The University of North Carolina Press, 2005).

[2] David Tyack and Robert Lowe, "The Constitutional Moment: Reconstruction and Black Education in the South," *American Journal of Education*, 94, No. 2 (Feb. 1986).

in the policy debates about how black students should be taught. Northern missionaries wanted to promote religious beliefs to newly freed slaves. African American political leaders were concerned with training a new cadre of leaders who could serve as role models in the black community. African American parents wanted African American teachers to replace the Northern white women missionary teachers who had typically taught African American children. And, the Southern political elite viewed the provision of education to former slaves skeptically, because of a desire to reinforce the caste status of African Americans.[3]

The heated passions of these conversations demonstrated the symbolic importance that black teachers held in a vastly reconfigured social order. Both newly freed African Americans as well as their advocates understood that literacy would be the path to gaining a foothold into American society and saw the hiring of black teachers as both a symbolic and a practical goal. It is in this context that the role of the black teacher came to represent the larger struggle for full political rights.

African American parents during Reconstruction advocated that African American teachers should serve African American students. Recent historiography about the education of formerly enslaved individuals makes it clear that African Americans used different types of institutional structures to advance a claim that their children should be taught by other African Americans. For example, in her recent micro-history of post-Reconstruction educational efforts, *African American Citizen's Council in St. Louis*, Melanie Alicia Adams emphasizes that by February 1864, African American men were requesting to serve on the board of the American Missionary Association educational mission in the city. This request ultimately led to the establishment of St. Louis Board of Education in the following year.[4] Likewise, in Savannah, Georgia, private institutions such as the Beach Institute thrived despite the challenges of raising money for tuition from previously enslaved African American parents.

This activism, directed toward increasing the number of African American teachers, belies the claim that formerly enslaved African Americans were not active agents in the development of educational institutions in the

---

[3] James Anderson, *The Education of Blacks in the South, 1860–1935*. (Chapel Hill: The University of North Carolina Press, 1988).

[4] Melanie Alicia Adams, "Advocating for Educational Equity: African American Citizens' Council in St. Louis, Missouri, from 1864–1927" (PhD diss, May 2014), 32–34.

Post-Reconstruction Era. Adam Fairclough, highlighting the beliefs of one education leader, notes:

> Bishop James Walker Hood believed that black children should be taught by black teachers. "It is impossible for white teachers, educated as they necessarily are in this county, to enter into the feelings of colored pupils as the colored teachers does", he told the North Carolina's Constitution in 1869.[5]

The African American desire for educational autonomy unfortunately coincided with the desire by a white Southern elite to reduce the presence of Northern school teachers, so they often worked alongside black families to remove white Northern women school teachers. Ultimately, by 1900 the majority of school teachers in the South were African American.[6]

Significant challenges existed, however, in creating the black teaching professorate, since at the end of the Civil War only 5–10% of the African American population was literate.[7] Beyond the challenge of raising literacy standards, African American communities often lacked the financial capital to fund educational institutions. Consequently, African American communities had to appeal to white Northern and Southern philanthropy to provide funding for elementary, secondary, and university institutions. This brought with it the challenge of competing ideologies. James D. Anderson noted in his book, *The Education of Blacks in the South, 1860–1935*:

> All groups understood that no system of beliefs could be transmitted to the millions of black schoolchildren except through the ideas and behaviors of black teachers. Consequently, during the early twentieth century black teacher training departments became primary battlefields for campaigns to translate particular ideologies of black education into institutional and bureaucratic forces.[8]

White Southern reformers believed that the purpose of black teacher education should be to produce rural school teachers who reinforced the white hegemonic social order in the South.[9] White Northern missionary

---

[5] Adam Fairclough, *A Class of Their Own: Black Teachers in the Segregated South*. (Cambridge: Harvard University, 2007).

[6] Ibid., 62.

[7] James W. Fraser, Preparing *America's Teachers: A History* (New York: Teachers College Press, 2007).

[8] Anderson, *The Education of Blacks in the South, 1860–1935*, 111.

[9] Ibid.

organizations such as the American Missionary Association (AMA) most prominently, as well as black religious organizations such as the African Methodist Episcopal Church, thought black teachers should be prepared within the "classical liberal tradition" to provide morally worthy instruction to their students. These competing desires often meant that the period between the Civil War and Reconstruction was ripe and fertile ground for serious discussions about how black education institutions, policies, and curriculum could be shaped.

Models of African American Teacher Preparation

Two models of teacher training emerged during Reconstruction to prepare African American teachers. The Reconstruction Era ushered significant bureaucratic experimentation in elementary and secondary schools. For instance, during the years 1865–1875, the Freedmen's Bureau began to establish public schools and according to one estimate [according to the article, "Secondary Education for Negroes"] established 4000 schools to begin to provide elementary education for African Americans the close of Reconstruction.[10] The challenge of creating basic elementary programs for formerly enslaved students to learn skills of basic literacy thwarted the establishment of comprehensive high schools until the early twentieth century.

The Missionary Experience

Missionary associations were often at the forefront of early educational efforts during Reconstruction. Northern white missionary organizations as well as black missionary organizations created missionary schools.[11] White missionary organizations included the American Missionary Association, the Freedmen's Aid Society of the Methodist Episcopal Church, the American Baptist Home Missionary Association. The Freedmen of the Presbyterian Church, African Methodist Episcopal Church, the Colored Methodist Episcopal Church, and the African Methodist Episcopal Zion Church were primarily run by African Americans.[12]

---

[10] Elias Knox, "Historical Sketch of Secondary Education for Negroes." In "The Negro Adolescent and his Education." *The Journal of Negro Education* 9, no.3 (July 1940): 446.
[11] Fraser, *Preparing American's Teachers: A History*, 104.
[12] Ibid.

The American Missionary Association (AMA) played a particularly significant role in establishing elementary, secondary, and higher education schools, as well as colleges and normal schools. By 1870, the AMA had established at least eight colleges and universities: Hampton Institute in Virginia, Berea College in Kentucky, Atlanta University in Georgia, Fisk University in Tennessee, Talladega College in Alabama, Tougaloo University in Mississippi, Straight University in Louisiana, and Tillotson University in Texas. By 1870, the AMA also operated several normal schools that had originated during the 1830s and 1840s in Massachusetts after a period of intense reflection about the role of public education.[13] A normal school's major purpose was a teacher training school, with an explicit training program that emphasized a curriculum of content and pedagogy. Consequently, the "normal" school was the first institute of higher education to deliberately eschew the liberal arts curriculum for a program that would explicitly prepare teachers to work in schools.[14]

The specific teaching training methods of the AMA normal schools, colleges, and universities appear to pivot on three different strategies. First, the AMA often combined its normal departments or normal schools with its elementary schools. For instance, in the *History of the American Missionary Association, With Illustrative Facts and Anecdotes*, the Association noted that the Hand Primary Building was erected at Tougaloo and that the building "accommodated three grades and is mainly taught by students as a practice school for the Normal Department."[15] Likewise, at the Lemoyne Normal Institute, in Memphis, Tennessee, the AMA noted that:

> The school consists of normal, grammar, intermediate, and primary departments. The pupils of the lower grades furnish practice and observation work in the training of teachers in the normal department.[16]

Second, the AMA sought to expose its students to a liberal arts curriculum at both its normal schools and colleges. For instance, in an 1866

---

[13] Anderson, *The Education of Blacks in the South, 1860–1935*, 99.
[14] Ibid.
[15] American Missionary Association, *History of the American Missionary Association: with illustrative Facts and* anecdotes (New York: January 1, 1891), 31.
[16] American Missionary Association, *History of the American Missionary Association*, 40.

report of then President William Hyde recounting his work of the Executive Committee, noted in regard to the instructional development:

> It is, however, not the quantity but the quality of the work done which is of chief importance. The great danger of educational work among enthusiastic by previously unenlightened people is superficiality. The tendency to realize at once an educational investment; the readiness to substitute a smattering of many things for a substantial grounding in essentials has been the peculiar bane of many schools for the colored race. Your committee note with satisfaction the evidence of thoroughness in the work of our chartered institutions. Not that it is the chief aim of our schools to provide their graduates with lucrative mathematics professorships, or supply Ohio colleges with Greek professors. But the fact that now and then a graduate of Fisk and Atlanta is able to take such a position is a gratifying evidence that the education these institutions are giving is such, not alone relatively to the prevailing ignorance out of which the students are drawn, but that it is education as measured by our own standards.[17]

This passage reflects the pride in which the AMA took in training its African American teachers to be equal to the students of equivalent white institutions. With that in mind, as noted by Hyde, the universities, colleges, and normal schools introduced its students to mathematics, Latin, and Greek—mainstays of what would be considered an appropriate liberal curriculum in the late nineteenth century. It also captures the extent to which these missionaries directly claimed that by exposing its students to the liberal arts curriculum, such a curriculum would foster equal conditions of citizenship for students that graduated from the students of missionary charted institutions. Indeed, it also foreshadows the pervasive concern of citizenship that also marked the many components of the alternative black curriculum.

However, it is the third element of AMA pedagogy which proved to be the most controversial: the combination of teaching training with industrial education. In a move that appeared to be initiated by former Union general, Samuel Chapman Armstrong, the AMA charted schools often advocated for a model of preparing teachers that forced teacher candidates to engage in a program that emphasized manual and industrial labor.[18] For instance, in its discussion of Talladega College in Alabama, the AMA

---

[17] American Missionary Association, *The Fortieth Annual Report of the American Missionary Association and the Proceedings at the Annual Meeting*, (New Haven Connecticut: October 19th–21st, 1886), 21.

[18] Anderson, *The Education of Blacks in the South, 1860–1935.*, 111.

History of the Mission Association noted that "industrial training has always had a place at Talladega" and thus, male students were required to take courses in:

> farming, gardening, wood-working, cabinet-making, carpentry, including repairs of all sorts, some iron-working and soldering, brick laying, printing and cobbling; and female students were required to undertake housekeeping, laundry-work, and nursing.[19]

Booker T. Washington, a student of Samuel Armstrong Chapman, later popularized the industrial focus of historically black colleges, claiming that the experience of work offered moral benefits to African American students. In his book, *Working with the hands; being a sequel to "Up From Slavery," covering the author's experiences in industrial training at Tuskegee*, Booker T. Washington articulated a complex view of industrial education insofar as he claimed that from an educational standpoint, industrial educational pedagogy was sensitive to the need to train teachers to combine intellectual and experiential learning opportunities for their students.[20] Specifically, Washington noted that teachers needed "industrial education" to offer pedagogical value to students:

> I have seen teachers compel students to puzzle for hours over the problem of the working of a pulley, when not a block for the school-house were workmen with pulleys in actual operation, hoisting bricks for the walks of a new building.[21]

Booker T. Washington, therefore, argues that industrial education offered a comprehensive ability to situate learners into an integrated learning environment. Moreover, industrial education, for Washington provided a way to bridge the skills of a formerly enslaved population to a more formalized educational environment. He noted that:

> We said that as a slave, the Negro was worked; as a freeman, he must learn to work. There is a vast difference between working and being worked. Being worked means degradation; working means civilization.[22]

---

[19] Ibid.
[20] Booker T. Washington, *Working With The Hands: Being a Sequel to "Up From Slavery, Covering the Author's Experiences in Industrial Training at Tuskegee* (New York: Doubleday, 1904), 9.
[21] Booker T. Washington, *Working With The Hands*, 159.
[22] Ibid.

Scholarly literature has been critical of the model of industrial education, despite Washington's complex treatment of industrial education. For instance, utilizing a Marxian perspective, James Anderson has argued that the AMA-Chapman-Washington model as an educational model simply reproduced the maintenance of the racial hierarchy of the South.[23] The Tuskegee establishment and the eventual ascension of Booker T. Washington as a recognized political leader of the Progressive Era prompted a debate between W.E.B. Du Bois and Washington that remains the seminal debate in black education history. Washington broadly justified an industrial education stance while Du Bois advocated for a deepening of a liberal curriculum. Notably, however, the AMA attempted to incorporate both models. The intense debate between these two intellectual giants again emphasized the power the teacher was given in the African American community in the twentieth century.

The County Training School

The major critique of the missionary schools was that these trained teachers were not capable of negotiating the political dynamics of the rural communities. County training schools, which served primarily rural populations, offered a more pedestrian function than the missionary institutions. County schools, for many Southern communities, served as the major educational provider until the advent of desegregation in the 1950s. Michael Fultz, in his examination of African American county schools, noted that these schools confronted imposing challenges including inconsistent teacher training, as well as significant budget disparities between black and white schools, which impacted the availability of appropriate salaries for teachers.[24]

Preparing teachers to teach in county training schools proved to be a continuing struggle during the period between 1900 and 1940. Three themes related to specific training emerge out of the scholarly literature. First, aspirational teacher training often included a significant experiential component. Fultz noted that philanthropic efforts in this area were generally directed toward rural communities with the services of a "supervising teacher." The primary benefit of a "supervising teacher" is that the supervising teacher could directly aid and support the county school teacher

---

[23] Anderson, *The Education of Blacks in the South, 1860–1935*, 11.
[24] Michael Fultz, "Teacher Training and African American Education in the South, 1900–1940," *The Journal of Negro Education*, 64, no.2 (Spring 1995): 196–197).

directly in the classroom.[25] Second, teacher training for county training schools generally followed an industrial education model. James Fraser has stated that "industrial education was a highly publicized aspect of the county training, but the choice to do so was likely a tactical response in light of deep-seated segregation in the rural communities." Fraser further notes that county training schools were often positioned in local communities to later become the high schools.[26] Consequently, the claim that teacher training followed an industrial education model may have been a way to advance political claims related to the provision of school services during the fraught environment of segregation. However, the strategic use of industrial education may have impacted its effectiveness as an actual type of teaching training.

Creating the Curriculum: The Curriculum of African American Teachers Schools

Teacher training during Reconstruction was, in many respects, foundational and highly experiential. Both public and private entities sought to increase access to basic educational services, including literacy and mathematical skills. Moreover, the basic model of industrial education also advocated for teachers to acquire skills consistent with the special task of teaching a formerly enslaved people.

The professionalization of elementary and educational teachers did not occur until the 1930s and 1940s. This emergent professionalization of teaching training in the African American teaching force resulted from two trends: increasingly sophisticated professional networks that introduced African Americans to a wider range of teaching techniques, and increasingly sophisticated educational curriculum. Initially, state and national teaching organizations provided foundational opportunities to African American teachers. In 1996, Michael Fultz argued that black state teachers associations also offered opportunities for teachers to grow professionally. Fultz posited that it was meaningful that "African American state teacher associations responded to the often miserable conditions faced by individual Black teachers with articles in publications that detailed

---

[25] Fultz, "Teacher Training and African American Education in the South, 1900–1940," 202.

[26] Fraser, James. W. *Preparing American's Teachers*, 109.

innovative techniques and proper pedagogical practices."[27] Vanessa Siddle Walker noted that these state and, increasingly, national professional associations provided teachers with a wide-ranging set of materials, including state curriculum studies, citizenship training, and descriptions of new teaching training activities.[28]

Moreover, this outside institutional influence in teaching was coupled with more directed efforts to provide black educators with an increasingly sophisticated curriculum. The debate over content in the social studies curriculum occurred in the 1920s and 1930s saw an increased attention to issues related to curriculum development. A representative monograph is *The Social Studies in Teacher Colleges and Normal Schools* written by Earle Rugg and Ned Dearborn. *The Social Studies Curriculum* represented the increased focus on teacher preparation during this time. Rugg and Dearborn conducted a comprehensive survey of the social studies curriculum of normal schools and teachers colleges (only Miner Normal School, Bluefield Institute, and Maryland State Normal and Industrial School represented the historically black schools on the list of schools surveyed).[29]

Initially, Rugg and Dearborn found that there was little curriculum standardization across the schools, although the traditional course sequence was centered around the history of the United States, Europe, and Latin America.[30] Moreover, Rugg and Dearborn noted that the content of many normal schools did not sufficiently distinguish between the methods course between elementary school and secondary school education, noting that:

> The methods course prescribed for history majors who must complete four years to receive a certificate in this field is the teaching of history and civics in the *elementary* schools, yet these majors are primarily students who wish to teach in the high school.[31]

---

[27] Fultz, "Teacher Training and African American Education in the South, 1900–1940," 196–210.
[28] Vanessa Siddle Walker, "African American Teaching in the South, 1940–1960" *American Educational Research Association Journal*, 38, no. 4, 751–779, 758–59.
[29] Earl U. Rugg and Ned H. Dearborn. *The Social Studies in Teacher Colleges and Normal Schools*. (Greely: CO: Colorado State Teacher College, 1928).
[30] Rugg and Dearborn, *The Social Studies in Teacher Colleges and Normal Schools*, 23.
[31] Ibid., 33.

Finally, Rugg and Dearborn noted that there appeared to be some contention about topics that comprised the social studies curriculum, as schools struggled to determine whether there should be a bigger emphasis on geography, sociology, and economics in the social studies curriculum beginning in the 1930s.[32]

Notably, the Rugg and Dearborn survey also demonstrated the changes the social studies curriculum had undergone since reformations made during the Progressive Era. First, the Rugg and Dearborn survey indicated that the commonly covered social studies curriculum topics included in the history courses had changed to cover the colonial period and the resettlement of the West through territorial expansion. Interestingly, a number of course curriculums studied the Granger movement, which focused on a progressive coalition of farmers that sought to change price-fixing by larger national companies. This appears to be a shift from the *mythos* of the Progressive Era social studies canon to the study of a much representative history.[33] Second, the Rugg and Dearborn survey indicated the emergence of a new subject: social studies methods courses. Methods courses included aims and objectives of history, collection and use of materials, teaching how to study history, use of textbooks, use of pictures, and testing resources for history teaching and dramatization.[34]

The Rugg and Dearborn survey also notably highlights that no schools, including historically black colleges, mentioned American Indians, Asian, Hispanic, or African American contributions to the development of US history. The failure of the social studies curriculum to consider ethnic identity as relevant content suggests the ongoing importance of the alternative black curriculum. In this vein, three prominent scholars, Reid T. Jackson, Ambrose Caliver, and Carter G. Woodson, advocated for changings in content and methodology that were consistent with the alternative black curriculum. Jackson, Caliver, and Woodson's are notable because their suggestions represented the emerging new role of the black education researcher. Black academic researchers began to produce knowledge which offered a more nuanced critique of the black education experience. And in an era of systematic educational inequality, these educational researchers' advocacy of a more nuanced assessment of African Americans was particularly important, as their work lacked the continual

[32] Ibid., 24.
[33] Ibid., 47.
[34] Ibid., 59.

racism common among white scholars during this time. Two topics were critical to this area of black education research: (1) a critical response to the claims of industrial education and (2) the need to create new types of teaching methods.

As discussed previously, *The Mis-Education of the Negro* is a central text of the alternative black counter-canon. *The Mis-Education of the Negro* should also be seen (and read) as an educational jeremiad about the development of institutions of higher learning for African Americans. Carter G. Woodson attacked the primary model of teacher training from the Post-Reconstruction Era with its attempts to find a balance between industrial education and liberal arts curricula. Woodson dismissed industrial education, noting that:

> Negroes attended industrial schools, took such training as was prescribed, and received their diplomas; but few of them developed adequate efficiency to be able to do what they were supposedly trained to do.[35]

He was equally critical of institutions focused on a more liberal arts curriculum, arguing:

> During these years too, the schools for classical education for Negroes has not done any better. They have proceeded on the basis that every ambitious person needs a liberal education when as a matter fact that does not necessarily follow.[36]

Woodson doubted that the institutions of higher learning were adequately training African American college students to be servants to the black community.

Woodson attributed the lack of clarity in the goals of higher education to the paternalist demands of organizations like the American Missionary Association and other white philanthropists, stating that "[t]he aim was to transform Negroes, not to develop them."[37] Woodson specifically believed that white philanthropists controlled the content of the curriculum by determining the content of the curriculum, thus removing any role for African Americans from its design. The invisibility of black voice therefore resulted in a student population that was woefully ignorant of

---

[35] Woodson, *The Mis-Education of the Negro*, 13.
[36] Ibid., 14.
[37] Ibid., 17.

the contributions of Africans and African Americans to their disciplinary fields. For example, Woodson argued:

> From the teaching of science, the Negro was eliminated.... Students were not told that ancient Africans of the interior knew sufficient science to concoct poisons for arrowheads, to mix durable colors for painting, to extract metals from nature and refine them for the development in the industrial arts.[38]

Woodson's critique was that post-Reconstruction education lacked a fundamental story of African American identity because African Americans were denied the autonomy to create thier educational materials. Like other elements of the alternative black curriculum, Woodson's focus on the autonomy of African Americans to determine their educational content serves as a subtle revision of the question of citizenship that permeated the debates of educational curriculums during the post-Reconstruction period. The *Mis-Education of the Negro*, for Woodson, was deeply pernicious because it left the Negro unprepared for broader acts of citizenship in a democratic polity.

Carter G. Woodson, consequently, advocated for an understanding of African American history to be the central premise of creating the "New Negro." In the final chapter of *The Mis-Education of the Negro*, he elucidated on the purpose of the Association for the Study of Negro Life and History, stating:

> The method employed by the Association for the Study of Negro Life and History, however is not spectacular propaganda or fire-eating agitation. Nothing can be accomplished in such a fashion. "Whom the Gods would destroy would they first make mad." The Negro whether in Africa or America, must be directed toward a serious self-examination of the fundamentals of education, religion, literature, and philosophy as they have been expounded to him.[39]

Ultimately, returning to his academic roots, Woodson believed that to improve education, African Americans needed to begin a fearless examination of their history. Woodson was not a firebrand for direct action and non-violence but rather advocated for the growth of the mind.

[38] Ibid.
[39] Ibid., 13.

The second teacher training critique that emerged in the 1930s was linked to the methods of teaching African Americans. Ambrose Caliver was a prominent commentator on African American education during the Depression Era. Caliver acknowledged the tremendous challenge facing African American educators. His perspective was less harsh than Woodson's. He wrote that African American teachers had to contend with meager salaries, problems of supply and demand in rural areas, inconstancies in certification expectations, and curriculum policies and practices.[40] He also felt that the teacher preparation programs were too departmentalized. Ambrose Caliver argued that in order to successfully reform programs of teacher education, schools needed to develop a philosophy of "Negro education." Caliver believed that fundamental to the Black philosophy of education was a more scientific approach to education. Caliver described what he meant by a scientific approach when he wrote:

> A science in which abstraction and contemplation have a place as well as objectivity and exact measurement. A science which does not ignore social cultures and forces, but which finds in them fruitful fields of operation. When science is thus conceived, knowledge will be considered as potential power for use in the solution of social problems and as guides to conduct.[41]

Caliver further viewed black teacher education programs were not focused enough on the scientific principles of efficiency and progress.

Reid T. Jackson's assessments centered on the curriculum of black teacher preparation programs. He felt that the curriculum and number of classes of students had hampered their ability to approach the craft of teaching reflectively. Jackson's work dovetailed with Woodson's critique about the inability for these students to serve the African American community. In creating the ideal curriculum, Jackson proposed that the Negro teacher colleges add a black history course to the teacher education curriculum. He stated:

> An entirely new course, "Education of Negro in United States," makes its appearance in the curriculum. Its justification is based on the fact that Negro

---

[40] Ambrose Caliver, "The Negro Teacher and a Philosophy of Negro Education," *The Journal of Negro Education* 2, no. 4 (October 1933): 432–441.

[41] Caliver, *The Negro Teacher and a Philosophy of Negro Education*, 441.

teachers know very little about the historical backgrounds and the present status of the education of the Negro in the United States.[42]

Jackson believed that greater self-knowledge was crucial to create teachers who might instill black students with a sense of culture and pride. In the modern-day literature of culturally relevant pedagogy and multicultural education, this early education scholars' belief that knowledge of history played an essential role in educating African American youth is echoed. Caliver also believed that to create a more well-rounded African American teacher, a focus on the history of African American education was critical. Caliver wrote, "it is lamentable how little most Negro high school graduates and many college graduates know about their own race."[43]

Although these African American researchers critiqued the higher institutions that trained educators, they still had hope for solutions to these problems. They envisioned an education system that would fully prepare teachers to nurture and support African American students. Inherent in each of these scholars' beliefs about African American teacher training was the idea that candidates needed to acquire a strong sense of black history. Each of these reformers argued that it was the responsibility of the African American teacher to learn their own history to work better with their students.

---

[42] Reid T. Jackson. "A Proposed Revision of a Two-Year Curriculum for Training Elementary Teachers in Negro Colleges. *Journal of Negro Education* 5, no. 4 (October 1936): 601–611.

[43] Caliver, *The Negro Teacher and a Philosophy of Negro Education*, 444.

CHAPTER 6

Dialogical Spaces: Innovative Practices and the Development of the Alternative Black Curriculum in Social Studies, 1890–1940

Black scholars in the late nineteenth and early twentieth centuries struggled for a forum to contribute to the public discourse. Excluded from major academic journals and positions, black scholars' research did not receive widespread public recognition or acknowledgment. Each scholar responded differently to the challenge of exclusion. Carter G. Woodson founded the Association of Negro Life and History, affording himself an autonomous organization to focus on the promotion of black history. W.E.B. Du Bois worked for historically black colleges and the NAACP. However, Du Bois struggled throughout his career to establish a stable scholarly community in which to conduct his work. Although black men's work never received the proper recognition from academia, black women's academic production was even more obscured. Black women's efforts to promote history in the areas of race preservation, commemoration, education, and grassroots mobilization did not receive the same attention as their male colleagues.

The alternative black curriculum reflected what I have traced in my previous chapters as the ongoing relationship between the theoretical principles that underlined the alternative black curriculum, which often arose out of institutional contexts of the university and national professional associations, and the practical context of the everyday classroom. This relationship was heavily gendered insofar as the basic principles of the alternative black curriculum (first publicly articulated by male scholars) were supplemented and even furthered by an ongoing dialogue with the pedagogical work of African American women school founders, administrators, librarians, and teachers. I have referred to this ongoing relationship as the dialogical space of the alternative black curriculum.

In this chapter, after briefly discussing the conceptual framework at stake, I will consider how black women leaders in individual and group contexts attempted to influence larger policy discussions on the history of the African diaspora. Specifically, this chapter focuses on how black women educators emphasized one specific curricular choice: the inclusion of Haiti as a key historical event. The use of Haiti throughout various curricula represents how dialogical spaces, nurtured and sustained by women, generated a comprehensive argument about the essential role that Haiti played in a specific American context.

Conceptual Framework

Key to my claims in this chapter is the continuing relevance of the concept of dialogical spaces, which I refer to broadly as the limited spaces black women sought to carve out between the fields of history and education where they could think, act, and be acknowledged for their academic production. These dialogical spaces allowed African American women to assert their intellectual autonomy in light of social pressures to limit their political activism in the development of education theory.

A dialogical space should be seen in multiple ways, as such spaces that could be constructed within the context of concrete physical environment, as well as imagined communities centered on nonspatial intellectual collaboration.

Dialogical Sites of Resistance

Physical sites of resistance were necessary in forming the dialogical spaces of the alternative black curriculum. Saundra Murray Nettles argued in her book *Necessary Spaces*:

> Many scholars make the important point that segregated African American schools, particularly in the South, were sites of resistance for those who sought racial justice through instruction in traditional academic subjects such as social deportment and the contributions of Black persons and communities.[1]

---

[1] Saundra Murray Nettles, *Necessary Spaces: Exploring the Richness of African American Childhood in the South* (Charlotte: Information Age Publishing, 2013), 75.

While Murray Nettles characterized these landscapes of resistance as critical to black children's identity, her theory has relevance for the adults within this landscape as well. Black women educators developed a narrative embedded in a communal context. These "dialogical spaces" therefore fundamentally shaped how and why these women wrote. Black women reformers built "communities within communities." In order for their work to be taken seriously, black women founded their own schools and clubs, providing them with the opportunity to dialogue about new narratives in the social studies.

Scholars emphasized how black communities viewed the task of "racial uplift" as a joint mission; supporting the acquisition of physical sites of resistance would lead to the creation of dialogical spaces of resistance. For example, in Tuskegee, Alabama Margaret Murray Washington [wife of Booker T. Washington] organized the Tuskegee Women's Club. The Tuskegee Women's Club built the town's first night school. Over time, as the curriculum developed in the night school, the teaching of Black history became important. Cynthia Neverdon-Morton found:

> In spite of financial conditions, the Women's Club continued to support the night school. The curriculum was broadened to include additional academic subjects, including Negro History. In fact, because the history course proved to be so beneficial, the women encouraged the teaching of it in day and night schools throughout the county.[2]

Black women school reformers intentionally created opportunities for adolescent girls to build their self-esteem and identity. In Virginia, educators founded a girl's club which explicitly sought to teach girls refinement and class. The "nation-building" work took place at a time when the black community was under attack from the virulent racism prevalent in the post-Reconstruction period. Black women education reformers realized quite clearly that they could bring their knowledge and expertise to construct built environments for learning.[3]

Angel David Nieves argued:

> For African Americans, the built environment provided them with the opportunity to physically celebrate or perpetuate the memory of particular

---

[2] Cynthia Neverdon-Morton, "Self-Help Programs as Educative Activities of Black Women in the South, 1895–1925: Focus on Four Key Areas," *Journal of Negro Education* 51 (1982): 207–221.

[3] Neverdon-Morton, "Self-Help Programs as Educative Activities," 207.

events, ideals, individuals, or groups or persons. Although Black women may not have physically built these spaces themselves, they often actively fundraised to generate funds for the schools, community centers, and churches. In addition to these physical spaces, black women created "dialogical" spaces where they could actively generate ideas to construct the alternative black curriculum in social studies.[4]

These dialogical spaces, which developed between these black educators, created the foundation of the alternative black curriculum. Here, the physical sites of resistance, embodied in majority-black schools, clubs, and churches, served a generative role in creating alternative venues for publication and dissemination of the alternative black curriculum.

I will also consider a space where black women met as a separate, equal group of colleagues. The collaborative group spaces served as a policy "think tank" where black women could push each other to think about solutions that affected the African American community. In this space, black women challenged each other to think about innovative ways to lead change in their respective local settings. The Pan-African spirit reflected in these conversations formed a foundational piece of the alternative black curriculum. Although these works did not become part of the alternative black curriculum formally, the symbolic nature of the site of black women's collaboration is essential to understanding the promotion of black history and culture.

Second, this chapter will assess the curricular choices of Addie Waites Hunton from a chapter in the report, *Occupied Haiti: Being the report of a committee of Six disinterested Americans representing organizations exclusively American, who, having personally studied conditions in Haiti in 1926, favor the restoration of the Independence of the Negro republic* (1926). This chapter stresses that these works reflect how specific curricular choices influenced how the alternative black curriculum was crafted in the dialogical space of activism.

---

[4] Angel David Nieves, "We Are Too Busy Making History…to Write History," African-American Women, Construction of Nation, and the Built Environment in the New South, 1892–1968," in *We Shall Independent Be: African American Place Making and The Struggle to Claim Space in the United States*, eds. Angel David Nieves and Leslie M. Alexander (Boulder, CO: The University Press of Colorado, B).

The Importance of Haiti

The inclusion in the curriculum of Haiti as key historical event demonstrates three trends that reflect the importance of dialogical spaces in the creation of the alternative black curriculum. First, the alternative black curriculum incorporated theoretical trends into basic content. For example, the consistent presence of Haiti across multiple authors demonstrated its centrality as a story of hope and persistence. Second, pieces such as Leila Amos Pendleton's *A Narrative of the Negro* reflect the important intersection of physical sites of resistance and the creation of the alternative black curriculum. Third, the publication of *Occupied Haiti* demonstrates the importance of dialogical communities such as the International Council of Women of the Darker Races, in the creation of the alternative black curriculum in social studies. These dialogical spaces were critical in the development of the argument that Haiti played an essential role in Black America's quest for freedom and citizenship.

IMAGINED COMMUNITIES: BUILDING INTELLECTUAL DIALOGICAL SPACES

In areas such as law and medicine, black women were often relegated to the sidelines. However, in the education field black women were treated as experts on issues related to the education of black children. The dialogical spaces that developed between these black educators created the foundations of the alternative black curriculum. Akin to the school sites which represented physical, tangible spaces, black women created intellectual "dialogical" communal spaces to generate new epistemologies about social studies for black children. On issues related to the education of black children, black women teachers and administrators exerted quite a bit of control. In these school and community spaces, women generated scholarly and academic work that directly influenced discourses about historical memory in the black community. It was through the synthesis of the academic work of male historians and the application of the pedagogy from black female educators that the work of the alternative black curriculum became real for children.

In the early development of the alternative black curriculum, Anna Julia Cooper served as a link between the scholarship of black males and the work being done by African American women. Anna Julia Cooper was at the forefront of elite black women leaders who shaped a response to virulent racism in the post-Plessy period. Cooper was best known for her book on the views on the nature of black womanhood, *A Voice from the South*.[5]

Unlike their male counterparts, black women leaders recognized that a vital part of the alternative black curriculum in social studies was the necessity of uplifting black girls. These female scholars recognized that by including narratives in history that ignited people's consciousness about the contributions of black women in history, the status of girls in a male-dominated society would improve. In the *Voice of the South*, for example, Cooper exhorted her readers:

> Let our girls feel that we expect something more than that they merely look pretty and appear well in society. Teach them that there is a race with special needs which they and only they can help; that the world needs and is already asking for their trained, efficient forces. Finally, if there is an ambitious girl with pluck and brain to take the higher education, encourage her to make the most of it.[6]

Anna Julia Cooper was the principal of the M Street High School in Washington, DC, from 1902 to 1906, and she was also the fourth African American woman in the United States to receive her doctorate.[7] It was in her role as a teacher in the M Street High School where she mentored a young Nannie H. Burroughs.[8]

Anna Julia Cooper served as an example of how African American women navigated the roles of classroom teacher and scholar. Cooper's confidence in her beliefs was "nourished by her sense of equality with black men."[9] School as a site and space of equality echoed throughout the work of the black women architects of the alternative black curriculum. In referencing the dialogical spaces between education and history that Woodson and Du Bois explored, we must understand that in the male-dominated world of the early twentieth century, African American women had to create a different space within which to create knowledge: Although

---

[5] Anna Julia Cooper, *A Voice from the South* (Xenia, Ohio: The Aldine Printing House, 1892).

[6] Cooper, *A Voice from the South*, 78–79.

[7] Karen Johnson, *Uplifting the Women and the Race*, 54.

[8] Maurice Jackson and Jacqueline Bacon, eds., *African Americans and the Haitian Revolution: Selected Essays and Historical Documents* (New York: Routledge, 2010), 142–143.

[9] Deborah Gray White, *Too Heavy a Load*, 37–39.

no black women's scholarship was as publicly recognized as their male counterparts, these early women activists envisioned new realities for African American students. In Cooper's precedent we see women were using knowledge to expand African Americans' visions of the African diaspora. In the revisionist curriculum, these early scholars sought to understand the similarities between the various communities that comprised the African American experience. Anna Julia Cooper did not receive her doctorate until the age of 67, which impacted the amount of scholarship that she subsequently produced. However, she set the precedent for being both a scholar and a teacher.

Scholarly Dimensions on the Life and Work of Nannie Helen Burroughs

In 1909, Nannie H. Burroughs realized her dream of opening a girl's school in Washington, DC. Committed to the three B's, "the Bible, the bathtub, and the broom," the National Training School for Women and Girls (NTS) sought to provide a place for African American girls to be educated and nurtured in a separate setting.[10] Burroughs's vision of industrial and vocational education was heavily influenced by Booker T. Washington and his vocational training school, Tuskegee Institute.[11] She believed strongly in the professionalization of domestic service, black women's most prevalent occupation after farm work during this era.[12] However, this outward vision of industrial education was also balanced with a strong belief in African Americans' civil rights, as well as a love and passion for black history.

During the 52 years of NTS's existence, Burroughs did not have to rely on large donations from white philanthropists; she instead utilized smaller fundraising efforts and contributions from working class black women.[13] Evelyn Higginbotham stated:

> Year after year black women, many without education themselves, regularly contributed small amounts of money enclosed in barely literate letters of support. By giving "pantry parties," collecting redeemable soap wrappers,

---

[10] Burroughs coined the term, "the Bible, the bathtub, and the broom," to emphasize the values in her schools' vision.
[11] Higginbotham, *Righteous Discontent*, 213.
[12] Ibid.
[13] Ibid.

and continually devising imaginative money-making ventures, black church women across the nation worked for the furtherance of their school.[14]

I define NTS as a "solitary dialogical space" (although it is difficult to imagine because schools are so populated) because of Burroughs's reliance on her black women networks, which afforded her the freedom to experiment with the type of curriculum her school could offer. She was able to design a school structure that could match her vision of how black girls should be educated. In this space, Burroughs experimented with how she implemented the alternative black curriculum. She fashioned an Annual Appreciation Day, a pageant and a course dedicated to African American history.[15] Burroughs's pageant, *When Truth Gets a Hearing*, was designed to provide black people with the opportunity to defend themselves against white justifications for racism. This pageant was not Burroughs's only attempt at writing. She also wrote the *Slab-Town District Convention*, a play focused on Christian morality and values performed in the 1920s. In addition, she served as the editor for *The Worker*, a missionary magazine sponsored by the Women's Convention Auxiliary of the National Baptist Convention, from 1934 to 1961.[16] Despite her many responsibilities and commitments, writing was a tool that she utilized to promote racial and womanly pride.

Scholarship on Nannie Helen Burroughs has focused on two areas. First, a number of scholars have outlined the biographical and social context for her educational philosophy. Opal Easter authored the most comprehensive biographical review of the life of Nannie Helen Burroughs to date.[17] She outlined Burroughs's roles in the women's auxiliary of the National Baptist Convention and the National Association of Colored Women, as well as the founding of the National Training School for Women and Girls.

Sharon Harley examined the social context of Burroughs's spheres of influence. Harley situated her work in the class dynamics that influenced Washington, DC, in the early part of the twentieth century.[18] She characterized Burroughs as an activist who advocated for the working class because of her own humble beginnings. Born in Culpeper, Virginia, in

[14] Ibid., 220.
[15] Taylor, "Womanhood Glorified," 390–402.
[16] Audrey Walker, *Scope and Content Note of Nannie H. Burroughs Papers* (Washington D.C.: Manuscript Division, Library of Congress, 2001), 5.
[17] Opal Easter, *Nannie Helen Burroughs*, 25.
[18] Sharon Harley, "The Black Goddess of Liberty," 62–71.

1879, her mother was determined to provide her with a superior education, so she moved Burroughs to Washington, DC.[19] Burroughs graduated from M Street High School in 1896 and hoped to become a teacher in domestic science. In her pursuit of a teaching position, Burroughs encountered discrimination based on her class and racial status and was unable to find a job.[20] Sharon Harley argued that it was this experience which led Burroughs to advocate for working women's education.[21]

Scholars also have examined Nannie Helen Burroughs's professional work in the education field, including her instructional leadership at the National Training School for Women and Girls. Karen Johnson compared the work of Anna Julia Cooper and Nannie Helen Burroughs in their educational philosophies and careers.[22] She concluded that Burroughs's work was more practical than Cooper's, given its basis in concepts associated with industrial education. Traki L. Taylor examined the role of Nannie Helen Burroughs in creating a school specifically to develop and uplift the self-esteem of African American girls. Taylor emphasized Burroughs's embrace of domestic education and its potential to uplift the self-esteem of African American girls across the United States, the Caribbean, and Africa.[23] Michelle Rief discussed Burroughs's founding role in the International Council of Women of the Darker Races, created by African American female educational activists after World War I to deepen their understanding of the histories of the countries of China, Egypt, and parts of the Caribbean.[24] Most recently, Sarah Bair provided an analysis of how Nannie Helen Burroughs implemented a curriculum that emphasized civic education and African American history.[25]

Unlike many black school leaders, Nannie Helen Burroughs had the freedom to implement a school vision that used black history to support and develop the identity of African American girls without the fear of reprisals. Although the work of the school was not considered as prestigious as writing a book, the work created at this site must still be acknowledged as a type of knowledge production. By disseminating complex scholarly ideas, women school teachers and administrators provided an invaluable service to the establishment of the alternative black curriculum.

[19] Easter, *Nannie Helen Burroughs*, 25.
[20] Easter, *Nannie Helen Burroughs*, 26.
[21] Harley, "The Black Goddess of Liberty," 64.
[22] Johnson, *Uplifting the Women and the Race*, 1–13.
[23] Taylor, "Womanhood Glorified," 390–402.
[24] Michelle Rief, "Thinking Locally, Acting Globally," 215.
[25] Bair, Educating Black Girls in the Early 20th Century, 9–35.

Mary McLeod Bethune and the Creation of a Policy Making Space

It is interesting to consider the figure of Mary McLeod Bethune in the development of the alternative black curriculum. She is a mythological figure in the history of black education. She is profiled in numerous children's books and the outlines of her biography are well known. Born in Florida, educated at the Scotia Seminary and Dwight Moody's Institute for Home and Foreign Missions, Bethune was attracted to work in schools from the beginning of her career. She began her teaching career at the Haines Normal and Industrial School under the mentorship of Lucy Craft Laney. Bethune founded the Daytona Educational and Industrial Institute for Negro girls in 1904. She went on to serve as the president of the National Association of Colored Women (NACW), served as an important policy maker in President Franklin Delano Roosevelt's "Black Cabinet," and in 1935 founded the National Council of Negro Women (NCNW). Of all the women studied in this book, she played the most active role in a policy making space.[26]

However, as one of the preeminent figures of the black community spanning the period of the development of the alternative black curriculum, her work in creating and sustaining black history has not been closely examined. She exemplified the notion of a black woman who moved easily through the dialogical spaces previously outlined. Mary McLeod Bethune served as an institution builder, a leader in providing black women a voice in discussing the creation of a black history curriculum, and finally as a writer and thinker in her own right about the meaning of history in the lives of black children. In her leadership of the Daytona Educational and Industrial Institute for Negro Girls, it was difficult to find evidence of a commitment to teaching black history like that of Nannie H. Burroughs. Bethune demonstrated expertise in fundraising which ultimately allowed her to merge her school with the Cookman Institute in Jacksonville. Her focus on industrial education ensured her legacy in higher education. Thus, as an institution builder, Bethune represented a conservative voice in the promotion of black history.

---

[26] Elaine Smith, "Bethune, Mary McLeod," in *Black Women in America: An Historical Encyclopedia, Volume I, A-L*, eds. Darlene Clark Hine, Elsa Barkley Brown, and Rosalyn Terborg-Penn (Bloomington: Indiana University Press, 1993), 115–126.

Conversely, in her work as the president of the Association of Negro Life and History, Mary McLeod Bethune embraced black history. In his relationship with Mary McLeod Bethune, Carter G. Woodson demonstrated that he valued the contributions of black women. It was through their relationship that Mary McLeod Bethune directly impacted the creation of an agenda focused on black history. Pero Gaglo Dagbovie explored that relationship in the book, *The Early Black History Movement, Carter G. Woodson, and Lorenzo Johnston Greene*. Dagbovie outlined how Mary McLeod Bethune increased the association's visibility, access to funding, and legitimacy and prestige within the larger black community.[27]

From 1936 to 1952, Bethune served as the president of the Association of Negro Life and History (ASNLH). According to Dagbovie, it was during the period of Mary McLeod Bethune's leadership that *The Negro History Bulletin* saw its most productive and creative period.[28] Because of her stature in the black community, Bethune was able to step into a policy making space as an equal to her male counterparts. Her legitimacy as a school founder, bridge between Black and White political leaders, and revered status among black women made her the epitome of the impact of black women in the social studies. Audrey Thomas McCluskey noted Bethune's ability to negotiate a variety of different constituents, and she argued this agility allowed her to navigate the complexities of educational landscape from 1890 to 1940.[29]

The least recognized portion of Mary McLeod Bethune's leadership is her speeches. While the authors of the alternative black curriculum focused their curriculum on modes such as pageants, lesson plans, and textbooks, Mary McLeod Bethune articulated a vision about the alternative black curriculum through her speeches and public forums.

Speeches

In a speech delivered in 1938 and subsequently published in the *Journal of Negro History*, "Clarifying Our Vision with the Facts," Mary McLeod Bethune made an impassioned plea for developing a vision for educating black children about their history. If one examines Mary McLeod Bethune's written texts, there is often a distant and cautious approach to

---

[27] Pero Gaglo Dagbovie, *The Early Black History Movement, Carter G. Woodson, and Lorenzo Johnston Green* (University of Illinois Press, 2007), 97.

[28] Dagbovie, *The Early Black History Movement*, 96–97.

[29] Audrey Thomas McCluskey, *A Forgotten Sisterhood: Pioneering Black Women Educators and Activists in the Jim Crow South* (Lanham: Rowman & Littlefield, 2014), 113.

her public comments. However, in a close reading of this speech, Bethune's passion for the topic is clear in her prose. She began the speech with a parable about the struggle for independence in the island of Haiti. In the story, Henri Christophe, a leader who played a key role in the Haitian Revolutions and the formation of government, defended himself to a British official who accused Christophe of trying to rebuild Haiti too fast. McLeod quoted the leader's passionate plea, stating:

> But we have nothing white men can understand. You despise our dreams and kill the snakes and break the little sticks you think are our gods. Perhaps if we had something we could show you, if we had something we could show ourselves, you would respect us and we might respect ourselves.[30]

Again, in her remarks, the vital role of Haiti in the formation of the alternative black curriculum is clear. She ends her remarks by exhorting the audience with:

> Today I would salute in homage that wise old emperor. I bring you again his vibrant message. Our people cry out all around us like children lost in the wilderness.[31]

After opening remarks, Mary McLeod Bethune made a nuanced argument combining a respect for the history field with a call to the black community to share their own history with pride. She argued that for every story that is offered about European history, Black people must learn their own history. She immediately pivoted into a discussion of the events of world history that related to African Americans. She highlighted the Pharaohs of Egypt, the adventures of Hannibal, and the stories of Alexander Pushkin and Alexandre Dumas. She made a comprehensive argument for a complex re-telling of American history beginning with Crispus Attucks.[32]

In one section of the speech, Mary McLeod Bethune equated black accomplishments with White accomplishments. Referencing the inadequate historical representation of Reconstruction by White historians, she said:

---

[30] Mary McLeod Bethune, "Clarifying Our Vision with the Facts," in *Mary McLeod Bethune: Building a Better World: Essays and Selected Documents*, eds. Audrey Thomas McCluskey and Elaine M. Smith (Bloomington: Indiana University Press, 1999), 212.

[31] Mary McLeod Bethune, *Clarifying Our Vision with the Facts*, 212.

[32] Ibid.

With *The Tragic Era* we give them *Black Reconstruction*; with Edison, we give them Jan Matzeliger; with John Dewey, we place Booker T. Washington....Whatever man has done, we have done—an often, better.[33]

This is a speech that is not given by a docile race representative, but rather a call to arms for black educators to teach a correct rendering of United States and world history. Finally, she connected American history with contemporary events. She quoted population statistics and the role of American labor in building American institutions. She also discussed the impact of black churches and the recent appointment of black judges. Finally, she lauded the decrease of illiteracy and the impact of Black education.

In contrast to the very public image of Mary McLeod Bethune, which is often portrayed as cautious and quite moderate politically, there is a freedom in this speech. Her passion for students developing a black identity was sustained by a love for black history. This speech was delivered in the latter half of the formation of the alternative black curriculum and echoed the themes and ideas of the prior writings of black women. Mary McLeod Bethune felt empowered and comfortable addressing a room full of male counterparts as an equal contributor in a policy making space. Mary McLeod Bethune's speech represented the apex of the impact of dialogical spaces in education.

Collaborative Spaces

The collaborative spaces that developed between black women and men were still very fragile because of the pervasive sexism during the early twentieth century. For example, during the Harlem Renaissance, key leaders, such as Alain Leroy Locke, actively discounted the ideas of black women.[34] However, because of their direct service work with black children, black women activists felt very comfortable engaging in debate about the direction of black education.

---

[33] Ibid.
[34] Pero Gaglo Dagbovie, "Black Women, Carter G. Woodson, and the Association for the Study of Negro Life and History," 38.

In 1922, a group of women comprised of prominent black women activists established the International Council of Women of the Darker Races (ICWDR) in Washington, DC. This organization, comprised of elite black women in leadership such as Margaret Murray Washington, Mary McLeod Bethune, Mary Church Terrell, Charlotte Hawkins Brown, Nannie Helen Burroughs, and Lugenia Hope Burns, sought to create a forum for education, political affairs, and social uplift.[35] Embracing Pan-African principles, the group extended the work of the National Association of Colored Women Clubs (NACWC) to include international scholarly dimensions. The purpose of the ICWDR was to connect the activism of African American women in the United States with women of color throughout the world. The group focused on education and uplift in Nigeria, Brazil, the Philippines, Puerto Rico, and Haiti.[36] The ICWDR served as a particularly interesting case study because of the organizational focus on the histories of black people in Africa, the Caribbean, and Latin America. The ICWDR, therefore, is a compelling example of how the emergence of the alternative black curriculum in social studies incorporated a diasporic vision in generating the development of curriculum.

The work of the ICWDR supplements this burgeoning literature on the black presence in the field of K-12 social studies/history. A theoretical focus on the work of the ICWDR minimizes a scholarly approach that has emphasized the social activities of the organization. Instead, this chapter emphasizes that the ICWDR performed an important activity in curricular reform by serving as a mechanism for black women educators to connect their work to other activities within the African diaspora. The work of the ICWDR represents a clear example of black women utilizing limited resources to provide shape to the question of what it meant to be a global citizen in the early twentieth century.

The early leadership of ICWDR critiqued the narrowing focus of the NACWC on issues dealing with black women's sexuality.[37] The ICWDR leaders sought to broaden the discussion to more political issues.[38] The ICWDR's most vital purpose was to provide a "dialogical space" where discussions could occur about how women of color could affect international issues. Since women were often excluded from venues of scholar-

[35] Michelle Rief, "Thinking Globally, Acting Globally," 203.
[36] Deborah Gray White, *Too Heavy a Load*, 37–39.
[37] Ibid., 39.
[38] Ibid.

ship, the ICWDR provided them with spaces to reflect, learn, and converse about the diverse nations of the world. The vision of these African American women represented the Pan-African spirit prevalent during the interwar period. The ICWDR contributed to the creation of a school in Haiti and formed study groups to analyze the conditions of women throughout the world.

The most successful portion of their platform included study groups to examine issues throughout the diaspora. Since the ICWDR membership consisted of educators, we can see that embedding an international dimension to their work was helpful to the membership. For example, there is evidence that as a result of Nannie H. Burroughs's participation in the ICWDR she became more active in incorporating black history into her curriculum.[39] Although the ICWDR folded by World War II, African American women's desire to seek understandings about the African diaspora is reflected in the alternative black curriculum in social studies.

The ICWDR promoted and disseminated black history through a variety of means, and the island of Haiti served as a special interest to the clubwomen. It offered a unique perspective on the events connected to Haiti because they were also interested in the impact of the historical and current events on the lives of women. Throughout its brief history, the ICWDR conducted a variety of activities that promoted a greater understanding of the island of Haiti. One of the early attempts of the ICWDR to conduct study groups focused on Cuba and Haiti. Margaret Murray Washington, ICWDR's founder, felt that by encouraging study groups, members could become more informed and further educate their own local communities. She once stated, "The first thing we are doing, is trying to get every [black] school, private, public or otherwise, Negro Literature and History."[40] Understanding the conditions of modern Haiti allowed members of the ICWDR to participate in larger policy discussions about the impact of World War I and racism in the larger African diaspora.

---

[39] Bair, "Educating Black Girls," 20.
[40] In her papers the first significant reference to a Negro History class occurs in the 1929 Student Annual. This reference corroborates with her increasing involvement with the ICWDR.

The Impact of Haiti

In the historical imagination of black people in the United States, the story of the Haitian Revolution proved inspirational during and after slavery. Early African American historical writers such as Martin Delany, George Boyer Vashon, William Wells Brown, and James Theodore Holly all explored the intersection between the Haitian Revolution and the freedom struggle of blacks in the United States. The Haitian Revolution was also studied in depth by the first African American woman to receive her PhD, Anna Julia Cooper.[41]

Cooper wrote her dissertation at the Universite de Paris at the Sorbonne on "The Attitude of France on the Question of Slavery between 1789 and 1898."[42] Included in her discussion was a reference to the events of the Haitian Revolution. Through an examination of the events of the Haitian Revolution, Cooper produced a narrative of a diaspora that reflected African Americans' continued fascination with the story of Haiti. Cooper, building on the earlier scholarship of W.E.B. Du Bois's work on Haiti, focused her dissertation on a comparison of the social conditions of the French and British colonies.[43] She published a book based on her dissertation entitled, *Slavery and the French Revolutionists 1788–1805*.[44] Her research on Haiti reflected the connections of individuals of African descent that were the foundations of the alternative black curriculum.

A second example of the impact of the Haitian Revolution occurred in the book *A Narrative of the Negro* by Leila Amos Pendleton. The centrality of Haiti in the alternative black curriculum in social studies can't be overstated. Pendleton began her chapter on Haiti with an illustration entitled, "The President's Palace in Port Au Prince, Haiti." Pendleton's history of Haiti started with a discussion of the Spain's role in the subjectivity of the Native Americans on the island.[45] She then discussed the period where both the French and Spanish occupied the island. She also shared a short biography of Toussaint L'Ouverture, emphasizing his leadership qualities. Finally, she described the modern-day conditions of Haiti. The chapter ended with the quote:

---

[41] Hall, *A Faithful Account of the Race*, 106–107.
[42] Johnson, *Uplifting the Women and the Race*, 112.
[43] Jackson and Boston, *African-Americans and the Haitian Revolution*, 142–143.
[44] Johnson, *Uplifting the Women and the Race*, 112.
[45] Pendleton, *A Narrative of the Negro*, 55.

How sad that the example of great Toussaint should so often be forgotten; Toussaint to whom Haiti was always the first and self last; Toussaint, true patriot, statesman and soldier of whom it has been said: "It is to affirm the scantiest truth that to the names of Cincinnatus and Washington, history has added that of Toussaint L'Ouverture.[46]

Toussaint L'Ouverture provided blacks with the mythological black figure whose intelligence and savvy allowed black slaves to overtake their French oppressors. Pendleton's emphasis on L'Ouverture aligns her with key themes of the alternative black curriculum in social studies. Providing an overview to the freedom struggle in Haiti, Pendleton also discussed the history and rebellion of the maroon community in Brazil and Haiti. Again, the emphasis on black freedom and autonomy is an important counter-narrative she explored in her work.

Addie Waites Hunton was born in 1886 in Norfolk, Virginia. She attended Boston's Girls' Latin School and Philadelphia's Spencerian College of Commerce. Ms. Hunton taught briefly prior to marrying William Alphaeus Hunton, who served as the first black secretary of the international office of the YMCA. In her post-teaching career, Hunton was a founding member of the NACW, she helped the YWCA start separate centers for women, and she also studied working conditions for women in North Carolina. In the black community, Ms. Hunton was held in high esteem particularly after serving as one of two women to work with black segregated forces in World War I. She published a book entitled, *Two Colored Women with American Expeditionary Forces* in 1920. In addition, she also wrote a biography about her husband, *William Alphaeus Hunton: A Pioneer Prophet of Young Men (1938)*.[47]

By the time Addie Waites Hunton assumed the presidency of the International Council of the Women of the Darker Races, she was well respected for her leadership in international and domestic affairs. Under the leadership of Hunton, the ICWDR continued its interest in Haiti. She, along with member Emily Williams, conducted two separate study trips to Haiti. In conjunction with the Women's International League for Peace and Freedom (WILPF), she represented the ICWDR on an education and study to understand the US occupation of Haiti in more detail. Addie Waites Hunton participated actively in the Pan-African Congress which

[46] Pendleton, *A Narrative of the Negro*, 64.
[47] Melinda Plastas, *A Band of Noble Women: Racial Politics in the Women's Peace Movement* (Syracuse: Syracuse University Press, 2011), 35–45.

occurred in 1919–1927. In fact, Addie Hunton and other black women raised over 3000 dollars to ensure the 1927 Pan-African Congress took place.[48] In 1926, Addie Waites Hunton and Emily Greene Balch co-wrote Chapter X entitled, "Racial Relations" which is an example of alternative black curriculum in its content and form.

Racial Relations in Haiti

Hunton and Balch started the chapter with an allusion to Haiti's historical past. However, the chapter serves as a more of a disquisition on race relations on the island in the 1920s.[49] For example, on the issue of colorism in Haiti, Balch and Hunton wrote:

> Among themselves there was a sharp division between the elite and peasantry, but it was not always an unbridgeable gulf. It was true that a lighter skin was recognized as an advantage. But there had always been men of distinction who African blood was unmixed.[50]

This quote demonstrates the importance of the alternative black curriculum in social studies attempting to tackle the impact of colorism on communities throughout the world. The authors went on to discuss the racial attitudes that US authors brought with them upon their arrival to Haiti. Finally, the authors considered the tensions between Black Americans and Black Haitians. They emphasized that there has always been a "tendency for Haitians to look down on American Negroes, whose slavery is so recent, and who are obliged to endure so much that it is humiliating."[51] This statement spoke to the complicated legacy of colonialism and racism between blacks from various geographic regions.

Although Hunton's and the ICWDR's work never appeared in the classroom, it is important to the alternative black curriculum in social studies for a couple of reasons. First, one of the key elements of the alternative black curriculum is complicating the traditional narrative of black

---

[48] Plastas, *A Band of Noble Women*, 35–54.
[49] Addie Waites Hunton and Emily Greene Balch, "Racial Relations," in *Occupied Haiti: Being the report of a Committee of Six disinterested Americans representing organizations exclusively American, who, having personally studied conditions in 1926, favor the restoration of the Independence of the Negro Republic*, ed. Emily Green Balch (New York: The Writers Publishing Company Inc. 1926), 113.
[50] Hunton and Balch, *Racial Relations*, 114.
[51] Hunton and Balch, *Racial Relations*, 120.

history. By emphasizing the history of Haiti, the black female architects of the alternative black curriculum connected US history to a larger global struggle. In fact, one of Mary McLeod's final trips abroad was to Haiti, emphasizing the key role that this small island played in the vision of the alternative black curriculum. Finally, by establishing a vision that encompassed the African diaspora, the founders of the alternative black curriculum were able to offer a gendered perspective to the development of a Black history narrative that transformed how Black children could access their history.

The ICWDR, in their work, sought to shape a discourse about world history for Black children in the United States. In the growing body of work on the alternative black curriculum in social studies, the content of the research has been primarily focused on the domestic context. It is likely, however, that my findings will demonstrate that there was a comprehensive discourse about world history as well. This chapter is significant because it lies at the intersection of three fields: American history, social studies historiography, and organizational histories of groups focused on international issues. The chapter is also significant because it links these three fields to an emphasis on how education historical method can incorporate a diasporic perspective in assessing the historical development of curriculums.

CHAPTER 7

Conclusion

The alternative black curriculum is still with us. During the school year 2011–2012, I attended the Black Saga competition. Black Saga's purpose is to "test students' knowledge of the African American experience as part of American history."[1] Black Saga is a state-wide event in Maryland geared to elementary and middle school students. Black Saga is attended by black, white, Asian, and Hispanic students, reflecting the diversity of Maryland's student population. By attending Black Saga, students were exposed to elements of the alternative black curriculum in social studies. Located in the Chesapeake Bay region of the United States, Maryland's rich black history lends itself to this type of program.

The actual competition day of Black Saga is the end of a learning process. While I was a teacher, my student interns and I worked with six African American girls to prepare for the competition.[2] My students tried to memorize 1000 questions about the black experience in the United States. My Black Saga girls did not necessarily take to the task with as much diligence as I would have liked; however, throughout the year they were exposed to a variety of facts about African Americans and the African diaspora. During the two years I coached Black Saga, all the participants

[1] http://www.blacksaga.org, March 16, 2012.
[2] During these two years, my student interns, Rhonda Humphries and Vassiliki Key, worked with me as co-coaches on the Black Saga team.

© The Author(s) 2018
A. D. Murray, *The Development of the Alternative Black Curriculum, 1890–1940*,
https://doi.org/10.1007/978-3-319-91418-3_7

were black girls. The ethnic backgrounds of these girls comprised a wide range of countries such as Panama, Mexico, and Sierra Leone.

At our weekly Tuesday meetings, besides learning about black history, we talked about how young ladies should behave, watched YouTube clips showing black performers such as Beyoncé and Nicki Minaj, and gossiped about the minutia of middle school. By exposing my students to the alternative black curriculum, my students' racial identity developed to include more knowledge about their own history. Each of the students talked about how they used facts about African American history in their own social studies class. So, much like Nannie H. Burroughs, I participated in the nurturing and development of African American girls. My mentorship might have been a little less formal than Ms. Burroughs; however, I understood that my role as their coach was to mentor girls who would serve in positive ways in our school. The Black Saga competition thus represents a modern-day attempt to continue to expose students to the tradition of African American history in the United States.

Intellectual Hybridity and the Alternative Black Curriculum

The experience of desegregation was a disruptive event in the educational experience of African Americans. African American teachers lost their jobs in large numbers. Many of the rituals that defined black students' experiences in schools were lost.[3] The tenuous presence of the alternative black curriculum today depends on our recognition that the alternative black curriculum has its own key narrative, as well as its own particular pedagogical techniques. This book contends that a conscious recovery of the conceptual and pedagogical techniques can be fully realized through instruction in social studies classrooms.

The existence of the Black Saga competition represents a modern-day example of educators' desires to expose students to the rich tradition of African American historical writing. Indeed, there is a direct linkage to the practices I have discussed in this book. The primary sponsor of Black Saga, Dr. Charles Christian, is a professor at Coppin State University. He is a tireless advocate for the teaching of black history in the state of Maryland. He also assisted in efforts to incorporate African American history into the

[3] Siddle Walker, *Their Highest Potential*, 4–5.

Maryland state voluntary social studies curriculum.[4] Dr. Christian's work embodies the central tenet of the alternative black curriculum—its accessible popularization of ongoing historical research within the field of African American studies.

As I transitioned into the role of principal, I've thought about the female designers of the alternative black curriculum frequently. As I embarked on this journey, I did not realize that these women demonstrated an intellectual hybridity that I have come to respect and seek to emulate in my own work as an educator. Their stories are my story. As a principal, I am working to lead a school that embraces a rich and compelling re-telling of American history. I face challenges of district, state, and national mandates that frustrate me in the implementation of this holistic vision for my students, similarly to institution builders such as Mary McLeod Bethune and Nannie H. Burroughs. Embedded in the work of the alternative black curriculum in social studies are examples of women that balance the larger issues of policy. Laura Eliza Wilkes, Anna Julia Cooper, Elizabeth Ross Haynes, Leila Amos Pendleton, and Addie Waites Hunton, to name a few, all exhibited characteristics of intellectual hybridity, including:

1. a desire to teach a complex and enriched US and world history grounded in the basic principles of teaching and learning
2. an awareness of the larger social political context
3. an innate desire to serve as a community builder
4. a commitment to publish and participate in the building of the field of K-12 history and social studies

Most of these women started their careers as teachers. This formative experience provided them with the experience to reflect on how Black children accessed and understood the experience of schooling. By studying the women of the alternative black curriculum in social studies that these women used teaching as a basis for developing a stance that influenced knowledge production in the field of social studies is clear.

[4] The Maryland State Department of Education formed a partnership with the Reginald F. Lewis Museum to write a K-12 state-wide curriculum. The objective of the partnership was to create a curriculum guide highlighting Maryland African American history, culture, and art. Dr. Christian also wrote a textbook on black history entitled, *Black Saga: The African American Experience: A Chronology* (New York: Houghton Mifflin, 1995).

Throughout the book, I argue that it is the responsibility of social studies to teach an enriched narrative of the history of social studies. I posit that black educators, in crafting the alternative black curriculum, built relationships with students through teaching them a history that is complex and embraced the richness of the black experience. The alternative black curriculum is by no means the only narrative about how minorities in the United States challenged oppression. Future historiographical projects in the field could study the possibilities of multiple discourses, such as the impact of Latino/Chicano counter-narratives in the 1970s and the continual arrival of Latinos to the United States.

The work of black female educators exemplifies a commitment to the broader political struggle. Too often, educators maintain a physical and emotional distance from the students they teach. The female architects of the alternative black curriculum understood that the work of educators is to raise children who had tools in place to fight institutional racism. They understood that teachers were not mere vessels of content, but rather that education was also an act of restoration in the task of rebuilding a free Black community. The work of the alternative black curriculum shows how teaching is intimately connected to a community-building function and current teacher preparation programs are missing opportunities to prepare teachers for this complex role.

Finally, the writers of the alternative black curriculum recognized the need to publish. Black women teachers used teaching to influence public discourses about how students should be educated. When historians examine the early historical writings of black women, there is no existence of a community. The striking, lonely image of Phillis Wheatley often comes to mind. However, this image is transformed by black women educators in the period from 1890 to 1940. From their position, they navigated complex relationships with black men and challenged the incomplete knowledge production of the Progressive Era. When Laura Eliza Wilkes on the front page of her book *Missing Pages in American History* declared proudly that she was a "teacher" in Washington, DC, she represented that in this role her voice mattered in the education of children. As teachers, finding our voice in a field which attempts to silence us is essential to developing an approach and commitment to address the poisoned rhetoric of current educational reform. Social studies teachers must develop their writerly voices in order to address oppressive schooling practices.

Racial Identity and the Social Studies

The emergence of the alternative black curriculum in social studies brings attention to the prevalence of race as a construct in a generation of new epistemologies in social studies. W.E.B. Du Bois viewed *The Brownies' Book* as a vehicle to popularize his complex historiographical rereading of Reconstruction and its aftermath. Such popularization would, consequently, instill a sense of pride for black students. In the advent of the twenty-first century scholarship in the discipline of social studies, it is important to consider how race informs how researchers design their studies and/or select topics to study. The formation of a student's racial identity is a critical component of how students learn in the social studies. In the last 20 years, educational researchers sought to provide shape to ideas of culturally relevant teaching.[5] However, to provide tangible pedagogies for teachers to implement culturally relevant teaching, it needs to be informed and supported by a discipline-rich approach. And to accomplish the goals of these approaches, the constructs of race need to be used in the research design process. By continuing to use race as a theoretical tool, scholars can refine their understanding of social studies to further measure student growth and achievement.

Black Women Pioneers in the Development of the Social Studies Field

Black women educators should be acknowledged as co-creators of the alternative black curriculum in social studies because of their work in creating "dialogical spaces" that refined the pedagogical and theoretical content of the alternative black curriculum. These dialogical spaces closed the distance between practice and theory. The representative work of this study, *When Truth Gets a Hearing*, embodies this dialogical space. This pageant represents a significant contribution to the literature of the development of the alternative black curriculum in social studies. In her integrated framework on race and gender, Evelyn Nakano Glenn called for studies which reevaluate the constructs of race, gender, and power as relational. She offers us a way to evaluate *When Truth Gets a Hearing*. A surface reading of Burroughs's work suggests a conservative vision of

---

[5] Gloria Ladson-Billings, "But That Is Just Good Teaching! The Case for Culturally Relevant Pedagogy," *Theory into Practice* 34 (1995): 159–165.

change, while a relational reading suggests its potentially subversive strategies for navigating a more complex historical reality. Moreover, a relational reading of *When Truth Gets a Hearing* suggests three key strategies for the construction of the alternative black curriculum. First, challenging the narrative. The creation of the pageant represented a black woman's reinterpretation of the dominant narrative in social studies. Second, model and reflect power and leadership. Nannie Helen Burroughs reinterpreted the dominant narrative within the school that she founded and for which she was responsible for determining the curriculum. Burroughs's students related to the material through Burroughs' leadership within the community. Her conservative message was coupled with Burroughs's creation of a separate, gendered space that placed her students into a relationship of power. Finally, the title of the pageant suggested that power could be questioned through hearing and counter-presentation. The pageant was a way to present skepticism about the popular historical narrative, and indeed, if performed in front of parents and other interested members, would offer this potentiality to the broader African American community.

As an educator whose work as a teacher has been minimized in the scholarly community, I relate to Nannie H. Burroughs. Much like me, she generated works for classroom practice that were ignored and obscured by the "academy" because they were not peer reviewed. Inherent in Burroughs's work is the tension associated with creating a curriculum in which learning can co-exist with educational activism and community building. The case study of Burroughs's work is about acknowledging practitioners' contributions to scholarly discourses about how to reflect and improve on practices in school. Black women in the education field searched to find a larger role in the "accepted" discourse of the education community. This tension between practice and research is one of the characteristics of educational research.[6]

In 1961, Nannie H. Burroughs died and with her death a very specific vision of how African American girls should be nurtured and educated faded. Nannie H. Burroughs aimed to create an institution with an intellectual curriculum based in a sense of community and racial pride. Her leadership exemplified how she attempted to negotiate a lofty vision with

---

[6] Ellen Condliffe Lagemann, *An Elusive Science: The Troubling History of Education Research* (Chicago, Il: The University of Chicago Press, 2000): 47.

the tedious nature of teaching and learning. In operationalizing the alternative black curriculum in social studies, Nannie H. Burroughs succeeded in one sense and failed in another. Throughout the period I studied at NTS, teachers continually conveyed the dominant narrative. As other scholars have noted, the dominant narrative in social studies is surprisingly resilient.[7] In fact, the evidence demonstrated that the dominant social studies curriculum was present at the NTS. However, through a course on Negro history, the Annual Appreciation Days, and *When Truth Gets a Hearing*, Nannie H. Burroughs succeeded in creating an environment where black girls received the opportunity to be exposed to multiple narratives. In fact, the story of her school is similar to the struggle which activist educators confront today: how to balance the needs of the dominant society with the needs of my black and brown children. Nannie H. Burroughs's willingness to take the principles articulated by her male and female colleagues and create a curriculum around them was a considerable accomplishment.

Chauncey Monte-Sano and Sam Wineburg, examining whether changes in curriculum materials have impacted popular historical consciousness, surveyed 11th and 12th graders about whom they viewed as heroes excluding presidents.[8] An interesting finding emerged. Martin Luther King, Rosa Parks, and Harriet Tubman were the most common popular figures mentioned in a range of student answers.[9] This finding demonstrates that a key goal of the alternative black curriculum, an accessible popularization of historical counter-narratives, has been achieved. In schools across the nation, students are demonstrating a broadened awareness of the centrality of African Americans in the narrative of American history. Indeed, the presence of Harriet Tubman intrigued most; she was an illiterate slave woman without much systematic impact on the ending of slavery. Wineburg and Monte-Sano attribute her presence on the list to the increased use of *The American Pageant: A History of the Republic* by Thomas Bailey with high school students.[10] In a recon-

---

[7] VanSledright, "Narratives of Nation-States," 113.
[8] Sam Wineburg and Chauncey Monte-Sano, "'Famous Americans': The Changing Pantheon of American Heroes," *The Journal of American History* (March 2008): 1186–1202.
[9] Wineburg and Monte-Sano, "Famous Americans," 1191.
[10] Ibid., 1195.

sideration of the major education movements of the twentieth century, the impact of the alternative black curriculum must be acknowledged. Bringing to light the obscured work of the authors of the alternative black curricula enriches and challenges conventional understandings of the evolution of black history into the social studies curriculum.

REFERENCES

Aldridge, Derrick P. 2006. *The Educational Thought of W.E.B. Du Bois: An Intellectual History*. New York: Teachers College Press.

Anderson, James. 1988. *The Education of Blacks in the South, 1860–1935*. Chapel Hill: The University of North Carolina Press.

Au, Wayne, Anthony Brown, and Delores Caledron. 2016. *Reclaiming the Multicultural Roots of the U.S. Curriculum: Communities of Color and Official Knowledge in Education*. New York: Teachers College Press.

Bair, Sara. 2008. Educating Black Girls in the Early 20th Century: The Pioneering Work of Nannie Helen Burroughs (1879–1961). *Theory and Research in Social Education* 36 (Winter): 9–35.

Bell, Derrick. 1980. Brown v. Board of Education and the Interest Convergence Dilemma. *Harvard Law Review* 93: 518–533.

Billings, Gloria Ladson. 1998. Just What Is Critical Race Theory and What Is It Doing in a Nice Field Like Education? *Qualitative Studies in Education* 11: 7–24.

Blaustein, Robert L., and Robert L. Zangrando, eds. 1968. *Civil Rights and the American Negro: A Documentary History*. New York: Washington Square Press.

Bohan, Chara. 2003. Early Vanguards of Progressive Education: The Committee of Ten, the Committee of Seven and Social Education. *Journal of Curriculum and Instruction* 19 (Fall): 73–94.

Brooks Higginbotham, Evelyn. 1993. *Righteous Discontent: The Women's Movement in the Black Baptist Church 1880–1920*. Cambridge: Harvard University Press.

Brown, Anthony. 2010. Counter-Memory and Race: An Examination of African-American Scholars' Challenges in Early Twentieth Century K-12 Historical Discourse. *The Journal of Negro Education* 79 (Winter): 55–63.
Brown, Anthony L., Ryan M. Crowley, and LaGarrett J. King. 2011. Black Civitas: An Examination of Carter G. Woodson's Contributions to Teaching About Race, Citizenship, and the Black Soldier. *Theory and Research in Social Education* 39 (2): 278–299.
Burroughs, Nannie H. *Papers of Nannie H. Burroughs*. Library of Congress.
Burroughs, Nannie H. *Appreciation Day Program*, Box 312.
Burroughs, Nannie H. *Annual 1929*, Box 312.
Burroughs, Nannie H. *Code of Professional Ethics*, undated, Box 311.
Burroughs, Nannie H. *E.J. Bonds Lesson Plans*, undated, Box 311.
Burroughs, Nannie H. *Etta Head Lesson Plans*, December 1, 3, 5, 1941, Box 311.
Burroughs, Nannie H. *Faculty Meeting Notes*, November 22, 1942, Box 46.
Burroughs, Nannie H. *Good Teaching Procedures*, undated, Box 311.
Burroughs, Nannie H. *History Tests*, 1920–1921, Box 311.
Burroughs, Nannie H. *Liberal Arts Division Schedule, 1946–1947*, Box 314.
Burroughs, Nannie H. *Miss Burroughs Appeals to Parents to Save Their Girls Now*, undated, Box 46.
Burroughs, Nannie H. *N.T.&P Teachers' Conference*, November 8, 1941, Box 311.
Burroughs, Nannie H. *Outside Activities*, Box 311.
Burroughs, Nannie H. *Our Music*, undated, Box 312.
Burroughs, Nannie H. *Second Semester Examination*, May 8, 1942, Box 311.
Burroughs, Nannie H. *Take Your Professional Temperature*, undated, Box 311.
Burroughs, Nannie H. *Teachers Reports, Fall of 1949-Spring 1950*, Box 311.
Burroughs, Nannie H. *Textbook Orders*, undated, Box 311.
Burroughs, Nannie H. *The Negro Project by Miss Gloria Dunlap*, Box 166.
Burroughs, Nannie H. *The Past and Present History of Germany by Miss Lorraine Shearron*, Box 166.
Burroughs, Nannie H. *When Truth Gets a Hearing*, 1916–1921, Box 47.
Caliver, Ambrose. 1933. The Negro and a Philosophy of Negro Education. *The Journal of Negro Education* 2: 432–447.
Carlton-LaNey, Iris. Elizabeth Ross Haynes: An African American Reformer of Womanist Consciousness, 1908–1940. *Social Work* 42 (6): 573–583.
Christian, Charles M. 1995. *Black Saga: The African American Experience: A Chronology*. New York: Houghton Mifflin.
Cooper, Anna Julia. 1892. *A Voice from the South*. Xenia: The Aldine Printing House.
Crenshaw, Kimberlee. 1991. Mapping the Margins: Intersectionality, Identity Politics, and Violence Against Women of Color. *Stanford Law Review* 43 (6): 1241–1299.
Cuban, Larry. 1994. *How Teachers Taught: Constancy and Change in American Classrooms 1890–1990*. New York: Teacher College Press.

Dagbovie, Pero Gaglo. 2003. Black Women, Carter G. Woodson and the Association for the Study of Negro Life and History, 1915–1950. *The Journal of African-American History* 88 (Winter): 21–41.
———. 2004. Making Black History Practical and Popular: Carter G. Woodson, the Proto Black Studies Movement, and the Struggle for Black Liberation. *The Western of Journal of Black Studies* 28: 372–382.
———. 2010. *African American History Reconsidered*. Urbana: University of Illinois Press.
Des Jardins, Julie Ellyn. 2000. *Reclaiming the Past and Present: Women, Gender and the Construction of Historical Memory in America, 1880–1940*. Ph.D. dissertation, Brown University.
Du Bois, W.E.B. 1913. *The Star of Ethiopia*. Series 12, W.E.B. Du Bois Papers. Amherst/New York: University of Massachusetts.
———. 1919. The True Brownies. *The Crisis* 18: 286.
———. 1920. As the Crow Flies. *The Brownie Book* 1: 23.
Easter, Opal. 1995. *Nannie Helen Burroughs*. New York: Garland Publishing.
Epstein, Terrie. 2008. *Interpreting National History: Race, Identity and Pedagogy in Classrooms and Communities*. New York: Routledge.
Evans, Ronald W. 2004. *The Social Studies Wars: What Should We Teach the Children?* New York: Teachers College Press.
Fairclough, Adam. 2007. *A Class of Their Own: Black Teachers in the Segregated South*. Cambridge, MA: Harvard University Press.
Fallace, Thomas. 2008. Did the Social Studies Really Replace History in American Schools? *Teachers College Record* 110: 2245–2270.
Fauset, J. 1912. What to Read. *The Crisis* 4 (4): 1–52.
King, L.J. 2014. When Lions Write History: Black History Textbooks, African American Educators, and the Alternative Black Curriculum in Social Studies Education 1890–1940. *Multicultural Education* 22 (1): 2–11.
———. 2015. A Narrative to the Colored Children of America: Leila Amos Pendleton, African American Textbooks, and Challenging Personhood. *Journal of Negro Education* 84 (4): 519–533.
Lepore, J. 2013. *Book of Ages: The Life and Opinions of Jane Franklin*. New York: Knopf.
Loewen, James. 1995. *Lies My Teacher Told Me: Everything Your American History Textbook Got Wrong*. New York: Touchstone.
Murray, Alana D. 2016. Considerations on the Alternative Black Curriculum in Social Studies: The Book of the Negroes. *The Journal of Social Studies Research* 40 (1): 1–2.
Nakano Glenn, Evelyn. 2002. *Unequal Freedom: How Race and Gender Shaped American Citizenship and Labor*. Cambridge: Harvard University Press.
Nash, Gary B. 2000. "The Convergence Paradigm" in Studying Early American History. In *Knowing, Teaching, and Learning: National and International*

Perspectives, ed. Peter B. Sexias, Sam Wineburg, and Peter Stearns, 103–120. New York: The New York University Press.

Nash, Margaret A. 2004. Patient Persistence: The Political and Educational Values of Anna Julia Cooper and Mary Church Terrell. *Educational Studies* 35: 122–136.

Neverdon-Morton, Cynthia. 1982. Self-Help Programs as Educative Activities of Black Women in the South, 1895–1925: Focus on Four Key Areas. *Journal of Negro Education* 51: 207–221.

Nieves, Angel David. 2008. "We Are Too Busy Making History...to Write History": African-American Women, Construction of Nation, and the Built Environment in the New South, 1892–1968. In *We Shall Independent Be: African-American Place Making and the Struggle to Claim Space in the United States*, ed. Angel David Nieves and Leslie M. Alexander. Boulder: The University Press of Colorado.

Novick, Peter. 1988. *That Noble Dream: The "Objectivity" Question and the American Historical Profession*. Cambridge: Cambridge University Press.

Payne, Charles. 1995. *I've Got the Light of Freedom: The Organizing Tradition and the Mississippi Freedom Struggle*. Berkley: University of California Press.

Perry, Theresa. 2003. Freedom for Literacy and Literacy for Freedom: The African American Philosophy of Education. In *Young, Gifted, and Black: Promoting High Achievement Among African American Students*, ed. Theresa Perry, Claude Steele, and Asa Hilliard, 45–88. Boston: Beacon Press.

Plastas, Melinda. 2011. *A Band of Noble Women: Racial Politics in the Women's Peace Movement*. Syracuse: Syracuse University Press.

Richardson, Willis, ed. 1993. *Plays and Pageants from the Life of the Negro*. Jackson: University Press of Mississippi.

Rief, Michelle. 2004. Thinking Locally, Acting Globally: The International Council Agenda of African-American Clubwomen, 1880–1940. *The Journal of African American History* 89 (Summer): 203–222.

Rugg, Earl U., and Ned H. Dearborn. 1928. *The Social Studies in Teacher Colleges and Normal Schools*. Greely: Colorado State Teacher College.

Rury, John. 2002. *Education and Social Change: Themes in the History of American Schooling*. Mahwah: Lawrence Erlbaum Associates.

Shaw, Stephanie. 1991. Black Club Women and the Creation of the National Association of Colored Women. *Journal of Women's History* 3 (2): 11–25.

———. 1996. *What a Woman Ought to Be and to Do: Black Professional Women During the Jim Crow Era*. Chicago: The University of Chicago Press.

Siddle Walker, Vanessa. 1996. *Their Highest Potential: An African American School Community in the Segregated South*. Chapel Hill: University of North Carolina Press.

———. 2001. African-American Teaching in the South: 1940–1960. *American Educational Research Journal* 38: 751–779.

———. 2009. *Hello Professor: A Black Principal and Professional Leadership in the Segregated South.* Chapel Hill: University of North Carolina Press.

Smith, Katherine Capshaw. 2004. *Children's Literature of the Harlem Renaissance.* Bloomington: Indiana University Press.

Snyder, Jeffrey Aaron. 2011. *Race, Nation and Education: Black History During Jim Crow.* Ph.D. dissertation, New York University.

———. 2015. Progressive Education in Black and White: Rereading Carter G. Woodson's *Mis-Education of the Negro. History of Education Quarterly* 55 (3): 273–293.

Taylor, Traki. 2002. Womanhood Glorified‖: Nannie Helen Burroughs and the National Training School for Woman and Girls, Inc., 1909–1961. *The Journal of African American History* 87 (Summer): 390–402.

Terborg-Penn, Rosalyn. 1998. *African American Women in the Struggle to Vote, 1850–1920.* Bloomington: Indiana University Press.

Tyack, David. 1974. *The One Best System: A History of American Urban Education.* Cambridge, MA: Harvard University Press.

VanSledright, Bruce. 2008. Narratives of Nation-State, Historical Knowledge, and School History Education. *Review of Educational Research* 32: 109–146.

Vaughn-Roberson, Courtney, and Brenda Hill. 1989. The Brownies' Book and Ebony Jr.!: Literature as a Mirror of the Afro-American Experience. *The Journal of Negro Education* 58 (Autumn): 494–510.

Walker, Audrey. 2001. *Scope and Content Note of Nannie H. Burroughs Papers.* Washington, DC: Manuscript Division, Library of Congress.

Wedin, Carolyn Sylvander. 1981. *Jessie Redmon Fauset, Black American Writer.* Troy: The Whitson Publishing Company.

White, Deborah Gray. 1999. *Too Heavy a Load, Black Women in Defense of Themselves, 1894–1994.* New York: W.W. Norton.

Wineburg, Sam. 2001. *Historical Thinking and Other Unnatural Acts: Charting the Future of Teaching the Past.* Philadelphia: Temple University Press.

Wineburg, Sam, and Chauncey Monte-Sano. 2008. Famous Americans: The Changing Pantheon of American Heroes. *The Journal of American History* 94: 1186–1202.

Woodson, Carter G. 1990. *The Mis-Education of the Negro.* Trenton: African World Press, first edition Associated Publishers in 1933, tenth edition.

Woyshner, Christine. 2006. Notes Towards a Historiography of Social Studies. In *Research Methods in Social Studies Education: Contemporary Issues and Perspectives*, ed. Keith Barton, 2–11. Greenwich: Information Age Publishing.

———. 2009. *The National Parent Teacher Association, Race and Civil Engagement, 1897–1970.* Columbus: Ohio State University Press.

Zimmerman, Jonathan. 2002. *Whose America? Culture Wars in the Public Schools.* Cambridge: Harvard University Press.

Zinn, Howard. 2003. *The People's History of the United States: 1492–Present.* New York: Harper Perennial.

Index

A
African American counter-canon, 64–68, 74–77, 81
African diaspora, 11, 49, 108, 113, 120, 121, 125, 127
Alternative black curriculum
  development of, 4, 6–8, 10, 20, 27, 43, 44, 47, 64, 66, 69, 72, 73, 76, 86–87, 111, 116
  as dialogical space, 108, 110–112
  emergence of, 19, 120, 131
  expression of, 4, 20, 48, 51–56, 117
  Haiti, 78, 118, 122, 125
  impact of, 11, 91, 102, 107, 128, 134
  intersection of, 11
  principles of, 3, 50, 64, 86–88, 129
  scholarship about, 18
  themes of, 9, 10, 79
  See also Counter-narrative
Association for the Study of Negro Life and History, 4, 68, 104

B
Bethune, Mary McLeod, 68, 116–118, 120, 129
Black Reconstruction, 63, 74, 85, 88, 89, 119
Black Saga, 127, 128
Black women's club movement, 2, 80
Brownies' Book, The, 2, 6, 10, 66, 69, 131
Burroughs, Nannie Helen, 112, 129
  collaboration, 69
  leadership, 6, 9, 20, 22, 23, 26, 44, 120, 121, 132
  NTS, 13, 22, 43, 113
  pageant, 48, 50, 52, 55
  scholarship on, 114, 115

C
Caliver, Ambrose, 10, 102, 105
Club women, 67
  See also Black women's club movement

Counter-narrative, 17, 19, 55, 63, 133
  See also Alternative black curriculum
Creation of knowledge, 7, 8
Crisis, The, 1, 66, 69, 73, 76
Critical race theory, 18, 19, 89

D
Dialogical spaces, 11, 108–112, 119, 131
Dominant narrative, 62, 74, 80, 133
  challenging the, 8, 17, 18, 44, 74, 77, 78, 82, 85, 132
Du Bois, W.E.B., 5, 6, 10, 20, 27, 47, 53, 63, 69, 72, 87, 107, 122, 131

F
Fauset, Jessie Redmond, 1, 69

H
Haiti, 11, 78, 108, 111, 118, 121–124
  Haitian Revolution, 78, 83, 87, 118, 122
  history of, 122, 125
  Toussaint L'Ouverture, 53, 78, 122
Harlem Renaissance, 1, 6, 71, 76, 119

I
Intellectual hybridity, 7, 129
International Council of Women of the Darker Races, 6, 11, 27, 111, 115, 120, 123

J
Jackson, Reid T., 10, 102, 105

K
K-12, 4, 6, 89, 91, 120, 129

L
Light of the Women, The, 10, 56, 58

M
Masculine bias, 5
Mis-Education of the Negro, The, 5, 10, 64, 74, 85–89, 103, 104

N
Narrative of the Negro, A, 1, 2, 76–80, 111, 122
National Training School for Women and Girls, 9, 13, 26, 43, 44, 52, 69, 113–115
Negro History Bulletin, 6, 10, 66, 70, 117
New Negro, 2, 71, 73

O
Out of the Dark, 10, 56, 57

P
Pan-African, 87, 110, 120, 121
Pendleton, Leila Amos, 1, 6, 10, 75–80, 83, 122, 129
Progressive Era, 3, 5, 10, 17, 65, 80, 86, 91, 99, 130
  education reform, 5, 6, 46
  historian, 62
  pageant, 44, 47–48
Public school, 1, 8, 11, 46, 64, 81, 88, 95

R

Race, 11, 13, 19, 23, 27, 46, 49, 50, 57, 61, 65, 82, 87, 97, 106, 112, 119, 124, 131
  racial identity, 19, 82, 128, 131
  See also Racism
Racism, 7, 18, 46, 53, 57, 61, 65, 79, 80, 84, 86, 87, 103, 109, 112, 114, 121, 124, 130
  See also Race
Reconstruction, 2, 7, 49, 59, 62, 82, 88, 92, 93, 95, 100, 118, 131
  post, 54, 56, 74, 91–93, 103, 104, 109

S

Sexism, 58, 80, 119
Social studies curriculum, 9, 36, 46, 62, 65, 85, 101, 129, 133

development of, 1, 4, 5, 17, 21
Star of Ethiopia, The, 10, 69

T

Two Races, 10, 56, 57

W

Washington, Booker T., 5, 10, 44, 56, 63, 81, 91, 98, 113, 119
When Truth Gets a Hearing, 10, 20, 43–45, 49–52, 54, 55, 57, 69, 114, 131, 133
White allies, 3, 57, 82, 87
Wilkes, Laura Eliza, 6, 10, 83–85, 129
Woodson, Carter G., 4, 5, 10, 17, 20, 27, 44, 56, 64, 69, 74, 85, 91, 102, 104, 107, 117
World War II, 6, 21, 32, 121

The manufacturer's authorised representative in the EU is Springer Nature Customer Service Centre GmbH, Europaplatz 3, 69115 Heidelberg, Germany. If you have any concerns regarding our products, please contact ProductSafety@springernature.com

Printed and bound by CPI Group (UK) Ltd, Croydon, CR0 4YY

23/03/2026

02076394-0010